Dirty Tricks Cops Use
(And Why They Use Them)

Bart Rommel

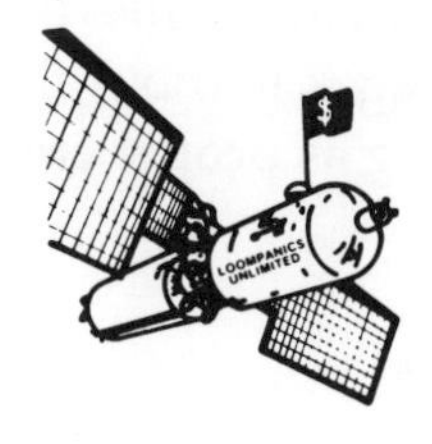

Loompanics Unlimited
Port Townsend, Washington

Other books by Bart Rommel available from Loompanics Unlimited:

- Execution: Tools & Techniques

This book is sold for informational purposes only. Neither the author nor the publisher will be held accountable for the use or misuse of the information contained in this book.

Dirty Tricks Cops Use... And Why They Use Them

Cover by Kevin Martin

Published by:
Loompanics Unlimited
PO Box 1197
Port Townsend, WA 98368
Loompanics Unlimited is a division of Loompanics Enterprises, Inc.

ISBN 1-55950-101-4
Library of Congress Catalog Card Number 93-77151

CONTENTS

Introduction

The struggle between police officers and offenders is unequal. Criminals have the initiative, and use it to stay one or more steps ahead of the law. In some cases, criminals are beyond the reach of the law because of jurisdictional problems or other technicalities. This is why police need to make the most of every opportunity to obtain arrests and convictions.

Police do not solve most crimes. According to the FBI and other sources, the clearance rates for most crimes are below 50%. The "clearance rate" is the percentage of crimes "cleared" by arrest. It does not necessarily mean that the criminal justice system convicts the suspect, or even that the suspect spends any time in prison after conviction. Murder, which once had a clearance rate of between 95% and 98%, now has a clearance rate of about 75%, according to FBI statistics. The burglary clearance rate, never high, has been dropping steadily during recent years, from less than 20% to about 13% today.

Even minor offenses are easy to carry out because the cops can't be everywhere. In fact, they catch only a tiny minority of traffic offenders. Ask yourself how many times you've seen other drivers dangerously violate the speed limit, run a stop sign, or drive in an erratic manner that suggests they were drunk, without being stopped by a cop.

One reason police solve very few crimes is that they remain unaware of them. According to several studies by the National Institute of Justice, people do not report most crimes to the police.

Part of the answer is, of course, better relations with the people police serve. "Community Policing" is one approach, and the final judgment regarding whether this will work or just be another buzz-word is still not available. In any case, this book is not about public relations, crime prevention, Neighborhood Watch, or other "soft" methods that enhance citizen-police cooperation. This is about heavy-duty enforcement against hard-core criminals.

Police officers deal with some very dirty and immoral people, who sometimes appear to have all the advantages because they know how to exploit every Constitutional safeguard to the limit.

This is the heavy-duty aspect of law enforcement. Officers' ingenuity can sometimes make the difference between "making" and "blowing" a case against a street-smart felon.

There are ways to redress the balance. Law officers have to use certain methods that skirt the edge of the law, and at times even cross over into illegality, to do their jobs against some of the heavy-duty offenders. A clean-cut and morally upright police officer soon finds that his Boy Scout mentality doesn't prepare him for encounters with street-smart offenders and sociopaths. To cope effectively, he has to become more flexible.

Criminal investigators have to be smarter and tougher than their adversaries. They have to have strong stomachs, and they must learn to make hard choices. Not every police recruit is suitable for this demanding work, and those with an inflexible Boy Scout mentality are best suited for patrolling parks and guarding school crossings.

Why this book? This is for the new police officer, who won't find this knowledge in any academy class. The small town or rural officer will also find these lessons from big-city departments enlightening. This book is also for the average citizen and taxpayer, to inform him how the police he supports really fight crime. The methods really used by police officers are sometimes as ugly as the crimes they combat. This information is also protection in case he gets caught in a police "sting." The unfortunate part about stings is that they sometimes trap people who otherwise would not be trying to commit illegal acts. Finally, the methods listed here are also adaptable for use by private security agencies, and not necessarily for legitimate law enforcement.

It's unfortunate that some police officers appear to concentrate on apprehending relatively minor offenders, and even innocent citizens, instead of hitting hard at heavy-duty felons. One reason is that it's safer to arrest a yuppie smoking a joint in his BMW than to shoot it out with a heavily-armed drug dealer. Another is the constant pressure for "production," statistics that help the police chief prove that his agency is doing a good job, and deserves a larger budget. A profusion of easy arrests looks better on paper than a small but select number of "quality" arrests.

Despite the best efforts of progressive police administrators, police work is still highly politicized in many jurisdictions. The mayor of one city urges police to hand out more traffic tickets to boost city revenues. The mayor of a small town tells his police chief to enforce the law, but "Don't arrest my cousin."

There are moral judgments to draw regarding police actions. The parallel with the military is close, because the military have to commit immoral acts for a higher purpose. It's their job to kill the enemy and destroy his power to sustain a war, even if this includes bombing his cities where civilians are targets as well as war plants. Bombing cities, done by both sides during World War II, took many innocent lives, including those of women and children. Courageous and dedicated airmen nevertheless carried out the bombings against determined opposition, in the belief that taking enemy lives, even innocent ones, would save the lives of their fighting compatriots on the ground.

Several international agreements forbid atrocities, and regulate the conduct of the military. Many of these are honored in the breach under the pressure of military necessity. Expediency rules that the military will destroy certain civilian targets, although random shooting of civilians occurs less often because it doesn't contribute to the war effort.

The scruples most military follow are to avoid wanton destruction, and not to make a personal profit from the war. Striking at civilian targets not vital to the enemy's war effort is outside the moral code, as are looting and rape. Many military won't condone unnecessary violence against civilians, because they have a strictly defined moral code.

The difference between police and military is that police officers are peace officers, and are not allowed the same freedom as military men. Those who enforce the law are required to follow it to the letter, both by the law and by their superiors.

Some officers use questionable methods to try to do a better job, risking their careers in the service of a higher good. Occasionally, police officers use strictly illegal methods to obtain arrests and convictions. Whether these are justifiable or not is often a gray area. Obviously, it's both legally and morally wrong to shoot a jaywalker, but paying informers with illegal drugs is not as clearly wrong, although it's always technically illegal. Likewise, planting evidence to obtain a conviction of a known long-term career criminal isn't clearly wrong, although it's illegal as hell.

Will this book help criminals? Not really, for two reasons. First is that criminals usually don't read. Instead, they watch TV or video cassettes. The second reason is that, for the criminals who do read, this book provides nothing new. Everything contained in this book was published elsewhere, usually in the daily news reports. Many street-smart career criminals have also taken the post-graduate course at what we sometimes call "the crime college," the penitentiary.

NOTE: This book uses the masculine pronoun in most discussions, defying the politically correct convention to use "non-sexist" language. This is in recognition of the reality that most police officers, and most criminal suspects, are still male, and that politically correct terminology such as "he/she" or "police person" is awkward to write and to read.

1
Image Versus Reality

Citizens from middle-class, affluent, suburban backgrounds may be surprised and dismayed by the harsh reality of the mean streets of crime, and what police officers have to do to obtain convictions. It's not like what they see on TV.

The media have always given prime-time treatment to law enforcement. During the heyday of radio, crime shows such as *The FBI in Peace and War* and *Mr. District Attorney* highlighted and glorified many law enforcement agencies. TV brought new police shows, such as *Dragnet* and *Adam-12*. Joe Friday, the laconic, moralistic, even starchy detective in *Dragnet*, always got his man.

Most importantly, he solved his cases by going strictly by the book. The two clean-cut, clean living patrol officers in *Adam-12* also fought crime and won, their morally upright Boy Scout demeanors an asset to their operations.

Some Hollywood movies are more true-to-life. *Dirty Harry* is an excellent example. Harry Callahan is a street-smart cop who takes no prisoners, and who is at odds with high departmental officials because of his rough-and-ready methods. The plot and dialog of each Dirty Harry film show that police administrators and politicians are more worried about their public image than about the realities of violent crime. Harry himself is a cynical, nasty, thoroughly disillusioned detective who understands that violent criminals understand only one language, that of force. He feels that violent criminals get off on technicalities and go on to victimize other citizens because of the ineffectiveness of the criminal justice system.

His solution to the violent crime problem is crisp and violent. His attitude, shown in the oft-quoted "make my day" scene from *Sudden Impact,* is that terminating a violent criminal on the spot is the only sure cure.

Real-life police officers, whatever their convictions, must keep a much lower profile than Harry Callahan. Even a "righteous" shooting brings an investigation of the officer and his actions, and in many cases an administrative suspension until the investigation has established that he acted correctly. A police officer who would dare to snuff the biggest crime figure in his jurisdiction would find that his superiors would immediately disown him, and turn him over for prosecution, because of the adverse publicity. Even a beating under questionable circumstances, such as the Rodney King incident, can have massive repercussions and break careers.

The tremendous positive publicity given to police by TV and by Hollywood doesn't quite cut it with many Americans, who understand that the real-life cops are not like the amiable and superbly competent TV cops. Street wisdom holds that "the cops are never there when you need them," a reflection of the police's inability to prevent or cope with many crimes. The increase in reported crimes, headlined in the press each year, suggests that police are less than effective in their duties.

One result is that many crimes never result in reports to the police. Despite the increase in reported crimes, reflected in the FBI's Uniform Crime Reports, the majority of crimes never get reported. The majority of crimes measured by the National Crime Victimization Survey, an independent study conducted by the Bureau of Justice Statistics of the U.S. Department of Justice, were not reported to police. The most highly reported (75%) crime was motor vehicle theft. The least (13.1%) was household larceny where the value of the property stolen was under $50.00.[1]

Overall, only 38% of all victimizations were reported to the police in 1990. The most common reason (20%) for not reporting a crime was that it was only attempted, and therefore unsuccessful. The next reason (14.7%) was that the victim reported it to another official. The third most common reason was lack of proof, in 10.5% of the cases.

Other reasons were that they felt the incident to be too unimportant, (3.6%) or that it was a private or personal matter, in 6.8% of the cases. In other cases, especially in big cities, people feel that reporting crimes is useless, because the police aren't interested (8.0%) or won't catch the perpetrators anyway (3.3%). Indeed, police did not respond to 14% of violent crimes, 33% of thefts, and 23% of household crimes.

One final reason citizens find that police image clashes with what they see on the streets is speed traps. Motorists ticketed for exceeding the limit by a few miles per hour on a straight road on a clear day may well wonder if this is optimal use of police manpower when more serious crimes are happening. Speed traps have traditionally been common in small Southern towns as a way of enriching the town coffers by fleecing Yankee tourists. This era is mostly in the past, but unfortunately, the practice has spread to other than impoverished Southern towns. Now that large cities in all parts of the country are using police speed traps to build up revenue, drivers should be aware of how to protect themselves. We'll take up speed traps in the next chapter.

Notes:

1. *Criminal Victimization in the United States*, 1990, U.S. Department of Justice, Bureau of Justice Statistics, February, 1992. Report NCJ-134126, pp. 100-102.

2
Speed Traps

Let's begin this study by looking at how not to do it. Speed enforcement, an aspect of traffic law enforcement that is technically easy, is a good example of wasted time and effort if the true purposes are to reduce violations and promote traffic safety.

The official "line" is that speed limit enforcement is to promote traffic safety. Actually, there are two basic types of speed enforcement. One is to promote traffic safety by slowing down or apprehending dangerous drivers, not only speeders, and taking extreme cases off the road by suspending or revoking their licenses. The other is to raise money for the police agency's parent body, city, county, or state, and this is known euphemistically as "revenue enhancement." The first objective is legitimate law enforcement. The second is abuse of police power, condoned and even encouraged by cities, states, and the court system.

One former state trooper maintains that hypocrisy pervades the system of speed enforcement, because police officers rarely get ticketed, even when on non-emergency business or even while speeding off-duty. Furthermore, in many jurisdictions normal driving speed is above the limit, and anyone driving at or near the posted limit obstructs traffic because other cars begin backing up behind him.[1]

Another hypocritical aspect of traffic enforcement is that many officers will extend "professional courtesy" to other police personnel, refraining from writing them tickets because they carry a badge. Chief Robert E. Shaffer, of Clarion, PA, condemns this "professional courtesy" because he points out that it's the moral equivalent of what we'd condemn as corruption in other occupations.[2]

Selective Enforcement

"Selective enforcement" is designed to enhance safety by taking down the worst offenders. Police officers stop only the worst speeders, such as those exceeding the limit in a school zone, and those weaving in and out of traffic lanes. They also stop those driving in a way that suggests they're impaired by drugs or alcohol. Selective enforcement involves patrolling stretches of road and intersections with high accident rates, and watching for drivers who speed recklessly, cut off other drivers, change lanes without signaling, run red lights, and commit other acts that lead to accidents. Such enforcement has to be selective because no police agency has the time or manpower to pursue all traffic offenders. Selectivity puts the emphasis on the dangerous drivers, and leaves the minor technical violators alone.

Revenue Enhancement

Revenue enhancement is another matter, and the tactics are very different. Revenue enhancement involves speed traps, and the reason they're called speed traps is that they're designed to catch safe drivers. A speed trap will most likely be on a quiet stretch of straight road with less traffic than main arteries, where drivers normally let their guard down because driving is easy. Speed limit signs may be obstructed by bushes, and the limit itself may change from block to block to catch drivers who don't pay strict attention to signs.

Radar Ins and Outs

A favorite tool for speed cops is radar, because a scientific instrument is intimidating to the suspect and carries more weight in court. This is the same reasoning that makes police favor the polygraph, or "lie detector," and the breathalyzer, although neither one is a reliable indicator of what it purports to measure. If it looks scientific, it's more impressive, especially to those who have a deep faith in "science." This is why the radar ambush is in common use. It's hard for a speeder to say that his actual speed was less than shown on the meter. It's also not a defense in court to say that the driver was being reasonable and prudent when the radar showed him exceeding the posted limit.

Normally, the 85% rule applies. This means that the speed limit is at a point where 85% of the drivers drive at that speed or less on that stretch of road. Setting the limit lower results in a great percentage of drivers exceeding it, because they feel comfortable at the higher speed. As we've seen, another trick is to post several speed limit signs on a short stretch, each with a different speed limit, so that missing even one sign leads to a violation. This generates more business for the speed cops.

Speed cops also depend upon psychology, which is why they don't set up traps where motorists drive defensively and are alert. They wait in locales where drivers tend to lapse into "condition white" because hazards are few. If possible, they set up at a point where the posted limit is lower than the speed at which most motorists drive that particular stretch. Sometimes, they have the help of the traffic engineer, who will post an artificially depressed speed limit to help the police.

Another approach to setting up a speed trap is locating the radar set over the crest of a hill. Drivers normally press harder on the gas pedal when climbing a grade, but any driver who doesn't back off the moment he gets over the top risks exceeding the limit as his vehicle picks up speed on the downgrade. Many drivers don't let up on the gas instantly, and speed cops know this, which is why they choose the reverse slope of a hill for a radar trap.

Another reason is that some drivers carry radar detectors. When a radar set is on the other side of a hill, its emissions, which travel in a straight line, do not alert a radar detector in an oncoming car until it's crested the hill and is within range. Then when the detector beeps, it's too late.

Yet another trick is to set up in an area with a lot of electromagnetic traffic, such as an airport. This makes it hard to detect the radar gun among other emissions, such as airport traffic. Airport radar covers the area by scanning, the antenna turning several times a minute, and the momentary pulse picked up by the radar detector sounds much like the pulses of modern radar guns with on-off switches.

The radar gun with a trigger-controlled transmitter is the most dangerous type. The officer aims it at his target and presses the trigger to turn on the transmitter, unlike the early and crude police radars which sat aimed down the road with transmitters continually on and warning anyone with a receiver that they were approaching the beam.

There are two types of speed measuring devices which do not depend upon radar. One is VASCAR, which has been in use for years. This is merely a time-and-distance measuring device. To use it, the officer selects a stretch of road between two prominent landmarks, and drives the length of the stretch at whatever speed he wishes. He pushes one switch at the first checkpoint, and another at the second. This measures the distance for the VASCAR's computer. Next, he parks where he can see both checkpoints, and when a car approaches, he pushes a "start" button when it crosses the first checkpoint, and the "stop" button at the second. This measures the time the car took to travel the distance, and the VASCAR's computer calculates the speed at which the car was traveling.

The second type uses a laser instead of radar. There are, at the moment, no laser detectors on the market, although this may change any day. The laser beam works just like a radar gun, but it's much tighter and much more directional. Using a laser, the officer can pick out an individual vehicle sandwiched between other vehicles, something radar cannot do reliably. Because lasers are so directional and tight, there's practically no chance of a speeder detecting one from far away, unless it's aimed right at him, in which case he's already in the trap.[3]

When cops stop someone for a traffic offense, they often ask casually, "Do you know how fast you were going back there?" or "Did you see the speed limit sign?" This isn't casual conversation. The officer tries to get the driver to make an incriminating statement to be used against him if he decides to plead "not guilty." Admitting guilt can make it much harder in court later, because the cop will record the statement in his notebook. A good answer, without seeming evasive or showing that the driver was not paying attention, is to say that he was watching the road, not the speedometer, because of a potentially dangerous condition ahead.

Quotas and Incentives

Officially, police departments do not have quotas for traffic tickets. However, police officers in Green Bay, Wisconsin, are protesting what they say is a departmental policy mandating disciplinary action against officers who fail to meet a monthly quota.[4]

Unofficial incentives exist. In Arizona, off-duty police officers can earn extra pay by conducting driver improvement classes. Arizona law mandates that for the first violation during each two-year period, the driver has the choice of going to court or signing up for a driver improvement class, which at the time of writing costs about $75. Taking this option keeps the violation from appearing on the driver's record. An added incentive for the first offender is that a recorded violation serves as an excuse for his insurance company to raise his premiums. Clearly, choosing the driver improvement class has benefits, among which are that the officer conducting the class earns extra money.

Coping With Speed Traps

The first and cardinal rule is to remain alert for ambushes and situations that may contain them. This seems like very elementary advice, but it's surprising how many people drive while paying only casual attention to their situations. "Situational Awareness" is the basis both for safe driving and avoiding speed traps.

Extra vigilance when rounding a bend in the road or topping the crest of a hill is important, because speed cops rely on surprise. A curve or down-slope can easily conceal a speed cop and his electronic device. Another favorite spot is in the shadow cast by a bridge or retaining wall.

For the many motorists who end up stopped by a speed cop, there's a right way and there are many wrong ways to prepare. A basic step is to look "clean," because first impressions are the most important ones. Police officers tend to treat with respect, or at least civility, the driver who appears neatly groomed and well-dressed, and who drives a clean car. A driver who hasn't shaved for a week, wears torn and dirty clothing, and generally fits the image of "dirtbag" is in for a rough time, especially if the seats and floor of his vehicle are littered with beer cans and other debris.

A clean appearance and polite manner radiate self-confidence, which is very important. This shows the officer that the driver isn't likely to be a suspect wanted for an offense in another jurisdiction, and raises the slight nagging doubt that the driver may be able to "fix" the ticket through political connections. It also may move the officer to give the driver the benefit of the doubt, and release him with a warning.

Many people increase their chances of getting a ticket by their demeanor. The worst ways to react to a traffic stop are:

- Be abusive or disrespectful. Insulting an officer will almost always lead to a ticket, or worse. In some rural jurisdictions, there may even be violence, inflicted while the offender is "resisting arrest."
- Claiming to know the officer's superior, or the judge, also doesn't work, because the person who really does has no need to try to negotiate his way out of a ticket with Officer Friendly. A quick phone call later can get the ticket fixed, and that's that.
- Threatening to plead not guilty and to "see you in court." This will only cause the officer to take extensive notes on the driver, vehicle, nature of the offense, and anything else that may be required during court testimony.[5]
- Hand the officer a fifty-dollar bill folded with the drivers license. At one time, this did work in some jurisdictions, such as New York City, but today many officers are too proud to accept bribes, especially such small ones, and will arrest anyone offering a bribe.
- Accusing the officer of racism, if the driver is a minority group member.

Talking the officer out of writing the ticket takes skill and luck. Drivers stopped for traffic offenses have only one window of opportunity, before the officer begins to write the ticket. The driver will make it or break it right then, while reaching for his license and registration. There are many ploys drivers use to try to talk the officer out of giving them a speeding ticket. One, described by retired Sergeant James Eagan, is the "potty ploy."[6] The driver asks the officer to hurry up with the ticket so that he may proceed to the next rest area to relieve himself. If there are bushes or trees nearby, another variant is possible. The driver leaves the car hurriedly and explains to the officer that he's got to attend an urgent call of nature. Few officers will follow a driver into the bushes to verify that he really had to go.

Another is for the driver to tell the officer directly that he depends upon his vehicle to earn his living, and that he already has enough points so that his license will be revoked or suspended with the next ticket. This appeal has to be delivered with a very sorrowful manner, or it won't work. The officer may write a ticket for a lesser offense, or release the driver with a warning.[7] But any attempt to blame the officer, such as suggesting that he'll be responsible for the driver's family starving, will backfire.

There is an excellent book that meticulously covers tactics for avoiding speeding tickets. This is *A Speeder's Guide to Avoiding Tickets,* listed in the further reading section at the end of this book.

Notes:

1. *A Speeder's Guide to Avoiding Tickets,* Sgt. James M. Eagan, N.Y.S.P. (Ret.), NY, Avon Books, 1990, pp. 1-7.
2. *Law and Order,* August, 1992, p. 101.
3. *Law Enforcement News,* NY, John Jay College of Criminal Justice, Oct. 31, 1991, p. 7.
4. *Law Enforcement News,* March 15, 1991, p. 7.
5. *A Speeder's Guide to Avoiding Tickets,* pp. 27-28.
6. *Ibid.,* pp. 46-48.
7. Author's personal experience.

3
Handling Suspects

A danger police officers face is that the next public contact may be dangerous and assaultive. An officer who stops a car for a broken tail-light may find that the driver is a bank robber who mistakenly thinks the officer is about to arrest him for a felony and opens fire. Although this rarely happens, officers have to act on the possibility that any public contact may become violent.

Nonverbal Cues

Street law enforcement is not like TV. Officers depend on situational, verbal, and behavioral cues for early warning of dangerous situations. Hunches rarely play a part in real life, mainly because tangible indicators are often present, and officers don't need to rely on intuition. The most obvious cases are "felony in progress" calls, and serving arrest warrants.

A person's ethnicity or apparent economic status may offer cues. This is why some police practice appears classist or racist, but is actually the result of strictly empirical street wisdom.

A black man walking or driving in a "lily-white" neighborhood is much more likely to find an officer stopping and questioning him than a Caucasian, unless he appears to have legitimate business there. A black dressed in a postal uniform, or driving a delivery truck, appears innocuous because he fits in and is unlikely to be stopped for questioning.

A shabbily-dressed person is more likely to be the object of a field interrogation than someone dressed like a bank president. This is the result of the practical observation that bank presidents don't stick up gas stations or commit burglaries. Another practical reason is that the well-dressed person is more likely to have connections "downtown," and may be able to generate "heat" for any patrolman who stops him without justification. This is very important in agencies in which politics plays a major role.

Race also is a factor because of crime patterns. The U.S. Census shows that blacks comprise less than 13% of the U.S. population, yet FBI Uniform Crime Reports show that 60% of the murders reported are committed by blacks. Similar disproportions apply to other street crimes. A New York State study by the Correctional Association of New York and the Coalition for Criminal Justice found that on a typical day about 23 percent of blacks between the ages of 20 and 29 are under the control of the criminal justice system — in prison, or on probation or parole. The corresponding rate for Hispanics is 12%, and for Caucasians, 2.7%.[1]

This does not mean that blacks are congenitally criminal, but simply that they are over-represented in street crime. Caucasians appear to be very prominent in white-collar crimes, such as high-level stock frauds and embezzlements, but these are not within the jurisdiction of patrol officers.

At times, police face a dilemma in ghetto areas. However, when they do, the residents may interpret this as "leaning" on them. This is especially true because crime is usually intra-racial, and police seek their suspects among ghetto residents.

In traffic stops, the officer routinely runs a check on the driver's license and vehicle registration. This usually includes a check for "wants," to determine if the driver and vehicle have any warrants or alerts out on them. Sometimes, this check comes back positive, and it's then necessary to arrest the person. It's simply not good police tactics to attempt an arrest alone, especially if the suspect appears to be a physical match for the officer or has a record of resisting arrest. If the situation appears dangerous, the officer will ask for a back-up to assist him, and play for time while waiting for his back-up to arrive.

Establishing and Maintaining Control

A police officer who wants to enforce the laws finds that his approach must vary with the type of citizen he contacts. It's one thing to write a traffic ticket for a grandmotherly type; it's another matter to stop and question a street-smart felony suspect. The officer can afford to treat the grandmother with kindness, consideration, and show profound respect. The brutal rules of the street require another approach with felony suspects, who often have a street-fighter mentality.

The street-fighter mentality is alien to many people accustomed to treating their fellow man with politeness and consideration. To the street-fighter, kindness is a sign of weakness, and he'll react to kindness by trying to exploit it. The street-savvy officer knows that, with this type of suspect, even if the suspected offense is trivial, it's imperative to establish and maintain absolute control of the situation by making it clear that he is "the man." This means conveying to the suspect that he intends to take whatever steps necessary to enforce the law, and that he demands respect.

In Los Angeles, a city with severe crime problems, one of the cardinal sins for a citizen is to show "contempt of cop."[2] Anyone who "disses" (shows disrespect to) a police officer risks some form of street justice. The underlying reason is not just cops' egos. If a police officer allows a person to treat him with contempt this is the beginning of losing control of the situation, because the suspect will keep pushing to see how far he can go.

The initial approach sets the tone of the situation. When stopping a well-dressed gentleman for a traffic offense, the officer may address him as "sir" and ask politely for his license and registration. The initial encounter with a scruffy suspect wearing gang colors and a prison tattoo is another matter. If the suspect asks, "Who, me?" the officer will say, "Yeah, I'm talking to you, asshole." Only by displaying a tough, no-nonsense, and even brutal, attitude, can the officer control certain encounters with dangerous suspects.

At times, suspects may actually be guilty but evidence is thin or not apparent to the officer. To avoid suspects' getting the impression that they got away with something when the officer finally has to let them go, the officer can do something to make their lives miserable. One tactic in car stops is to surreptitiously spray Mace into the dashboard and air conditioner vents. When the suspect resumes his interrupted journey, he'll get a healthy dose of tear gas.[3]

A variation on this theme works especially well when the car has fleece seat covers, or at least cloth seats. Spraying Mace into the fleece or fabric produces a long-lasting effect, because body heat causes the active ingredient, chloroacetophenone, to vaporize and irritate the suspect's bottom and crotch. CN, as chloroacetophenone is called for short, produces a long-lasting burning sensation, and is very hard to remove from the seat.

Finding Fugitives

Normally, it's not necessary to use such elaborate ruses to corral a fugitive. A standard procedure is to locate the suspect first, then decide upon the best way to apprehend him or her. We have to remember that many outstanding warrants are not for armed and dangerous fugitives, but for traffic scofflaws, fathers delinquent in child support payments, and other miscellaneous, non-violent crimes. Many people with outstanding warrants don't make a determined effort to evade the law, hoping only that it won't catch up with them.

A basic step is to interview the suspect's landlord and/or neighbors to determine if anyone can provide a forwarding address. Another step is to send him a registered letter, with a "show address where delivered" tag. In cities with city-owned utility companies, it may be possible to trace a suspect by the latest address listed with the utility department. However, some apartments offer utilities included in the rent, and renters' names never appear on any utility bill.

Yet another way to trace a wanted person is by canvassing his relatives and known associates. Some will feel obligated to cooperate with the police, and will provide his whereabouts.[4]

At times, officers have one or more likely addresses for the fugitive, but have trouble laying hands on him. Arresting a fugitive requires that officers and suspect be at the same place at the same time, and their movements often don't coincide. An example is the wanted person who holds a job, and sleeps at his parents' home. The simple way of making contact is to pick a time after the fugitive comes home from work.

When there's more than one possible address, the arresting officers must try to locate the suspect's current location. The telephone can be very useful. A few calls may pinpoint the suspect. Simply asking to speak with him will disclose whether he's at a particular place.

Street-smart suspects move around a lot, and evade surveillance by making their movements unpredictable. One way of coping with this tactic is for the officer to telephone the suspect's home and leave a message to call him on a pager number: "Hey, this is Mike. Have Jackie call me at 123-4567." Some officers use an additional ruse to motivate the suspect into returning the call, stating that they owe the suspect money and would like to pay him back.

The pager serves as a "cut-out," a way of making contact without revealing the officer's true identity or location, which might be around the corner from the suspect's address. Officers with cellular phones can place calls while keeping the premises under observation. The pager displays the number where the officer may return the call, and if this number corresponds to one of the suspect's known locations, it pinpoints him. If the officer is nearby, he can be there in a minute.

If none of these methods work, it still may be possible to trace an individual through his employment. Although a particular person may no longer be at the employer listed on police and court paperwork, canvassing employers in the same field can be productive. This isn't as complicated as it might seem. Restaurant workers, for example, have only a manageable number of employment possibilities in all but the largest cities. Telephoning restaurants may disclose the suspect's location if the officer knows that the suspect is working under his own name, or knows his alias. If not, canvassing restaurants is necessary.

Moving Surveillance

In some cases, it's necessary to shadow a suspect, a suspect's relative, or an associate, to find the target. A suspect may lead investigators to other wanted suspects. Crafty officers must use a variety of tricks to keep the target from knowing he's being shadowed. The most important one is "breaking the profile," changing superficial appearance by donning or removing a coat or hat. This is vital when circumstances force an officer to shadow a suspect without back-up. An excellent portrayal of this technique is in the film *The French Connection,* in which Gene Hackman follows a suspect through the streets and subways of New York. The depiction is so realistic that *The French Connection* is a good training film on this and other aspects of surveillance. The opening scene, showing a detective dressed as Santa Claus, is also true-to-life.

With a surveillance team, a variety of disguises and ruses becomes possible. Rotating the lead man in a close tail is standard, to minimize the danger of a suspect's "making" him. A stockpile of work clothing and uniforms helps shadowers blend in with the locale. Dressed as postal workers, telephone company employees, and in season, Santa Claus, shadowers can shadow or stake out a suspect while appearing to be part of the milieu.

Conducting vehicle surveillance at night can be very difficult, especially in a heavily-traveled locale, because the suspect vehicle's tail lights blend in with those of other vehicles. Agencies large enough to afford one of the electronic "bugs" that officers can attach to the target vehicle can easily follow a suspect, but smaller agencies don't have all the luxuries and must depend on traditional methods. One cheap and dirty way of making the target vehicle's tail light pattern distinctive is to break one. Keeping track of a vehicle with only one tail light is easier, and trailing officers can hang back to prevent being "made" by the suspect without fear of losing him.

Arrest Tactics

Arresting felony suspects can be both difficult and dangerous. Although the technique of surrounding a house with armed officers and ordering the suspect out via a bullhorn is dramatic, it belongs in Hollywood, and not in real life. Police officers prefer to make arrests without violence, if possible, because once violence starts, it can escalate very quickly.

Avoiding injury while making an arrest is important to the officer, who logically wants to go home safely at the end of his shift. This is why the element of surprise is a vital part of many arrests. To attain surprise, it's often necessary to use deception.

In felony warrant arrests, taking the suspect out of his home or stronghold, or out of a crowded room is the first step. There are many ploys to trick suspects into leaving their lairs. One officer, serving an arrest warrant on a suspect attending class in a trade school, had the school administrator send a message to the suspect to come to the office for a long-distance phone call. When the suspect came out of the classroom door, the officer and his partner were waiting on either side, and wrestled the suspect down to the floor and handcuffed him before he could resist.

Sometimes, capturing a suspect alive is the highest priority, even at the risk of officers' lives, because of the information they may obtain from him. FBI agents arresting John Walker, the traitor who handed over U.S. Navy cryptographic materials to the Soviets, knew that he had a lot of information pertaining to the materials he'd passed to the Soviets during his twenty-year career as a traitor. Finding out exactly what he'd revealed to his contacts would enable the government to assess the damage he'd done, which is why the FBI had determined that they needed him alive.

Walker had rented a room at the Ramada Inn in Rockville, Maryland. The previous afternoon, he had attempted to leave material for his Soviet contact at a dead drop nearby. To arrest him, FBI agents decided to trick him out of his hotel room. An agent, William Wang, posing as the desk clerk telephoned his room shortly after three A.M. to tell him his new van had been hit by a drunk in the parking lot. Agents Robert W. Hunter and James Kolouch, wearing body armor, waited for him in the hallway. When Walker emerged from his room, he was carrying a small revolver, and he became suspicious of the two men who were standing by the elevator at that early hour. He drew his gun, and after a short face-down with the agents, obeyed their order to surrender.[5]

Special arrest teams have other ways to get suspects to open the door, and even come out to talk to them. One is the "pizza man" trick, in which an officer knocks on the door and says he has a pizza for the suspect. If there's more than one person on the premises, the one answering the door may think someone else ordered the pizza.

One special anti-crime unit developed other techniques. One was to ring the suspect's bell and ask him if he was willing to sell a boat in his driveway. This lured the suspect out of his house to where officers could put their hands on him.[6]

Another trick to stop and apprehend a felony suspect driving in a vehicle is to have a marked unit make what appears to be a traffic stop. Once the suspect stops his vehicle, officers will either get him to leave his car on a pretext, or come up on both sides of his vehicle with guns drawn.

Fugitive detail officers can be very imaginative in luring suspects to where they can make mass arrests. In Corunna, Michigan, a fake wedding was set up by several police agencies to lure drug dealers to where they could be arrested. The fake bride and groom played roles as organized crime figures, and another officer played the clergyman. Several officers were the band, which played at the reception.

Preparations were elaborate. There were even matchbooks engraved with the names of the bride and groom. Police rented a hall for the September 21, 1990 affair, and invited suspected drug dealers. At the door, ushers asked the guests to check their weapons. At a signal, police officers arrested the guests.[7]

Bending The Rules

In certain cases, officers technically neglect their duty when common sense tells them that discretion is the wiser course. The principle of "discretionary justice" is traditional among police, and it has a sound basis in "street smarts." An example is the officer who stopped two men in a high-crime neighborhood and ordered them to lean against a wall for a search. One of the men told the officer that he had a knife in his pocket before the officer began searching him. The officer took the knife, and told the man he intended to confiscate it, because it was a concealed weapon. Under the law, he could have made an arrest on that charge, but the cop felt that confiscation solved the problem. The man, however, told him that he carried the knife for protection, because of the high crime threat. He added that he would continue to carry a weapon, because the alternative was to be confined to his home. The officer, upon hearing this, shrugged and gave back the knife.[8]

Police do not arrest suspects at every opportunity. They allow certain illegal activities to continue because those conducting them provide help and information they need. Any experienced beat cop knows that prostitutes often know more about what's really happening on the beat than the officer, and he milks them for information. Allowing the hookers to ply their trade, at least until businessmen and church groups complain, is mutually beneficial. So is tolerating other illegal enterprises. Although technically illegal, certain activities are far less harmful than others. To a street cop, it makes sense to assign priorities, and milk an illegal source for information regarding far more dangerous criminals. We'll study this in the chapter on informers. Philadelphia police allowed a gypsy cab operation to continue because the drivers gave them "tips."[9]

Another tactic works to keep an arrested suspect from contact with his attorney, family, and associates by shifting him from one holding tank or station house to another.[10] An attorney with an order of habeas corpus can't serve it until he physically locates his client. A police agency with many police stations can move the suspect irregularly from one to another, eluding the attorney. Small-agency officers can do the same thing by moving a suspect to the next town, or to the county sheriff's jail, making the rounds for as long as it takes to make the suspect feel isolated and to elicit a confession.

Fugitives in foreign countries are recoverable only by extradition, but this is merely the law, not actual practice, in some cases. When there exist good relations between American police officers and those in another country, it's possible to waive the rules and short-circuit the laborious extradition process. American and Mexican authorities have co-operated closely in certain cases. When Morton Sobell, a member of the Rosenberg spy ring, took himself and his family over the border to Mexico in 1950, the FBI took steps to recover him. On August 16, 1950, Mexican security police arrested him as an undesirable alien. Sobell did not go willingly, and officers struck him on the head before bundling him into their car. Another squad of officers gathered up Sobell's family and their luggage, and police drove them to the border at Laredo, Texas, in a convoy. At the border, Mexican police simply told them to walk across to where FBI agents were waiting.[11]

Federal agents aren't the only ones to obtain cooperation from Mexican police. California police agencies have also made use of the Mexican police's method of de facto extradition, which avoids formalities such as warrants, courts, and lawyers. Mexican officers simply take custody of the fugitive and transport him to the border crossing where American officers will be waiting. Then they simply release him and order him to walk north.[12]

Arranging such an informal deportation in a manner convenient to both police agencies requires finesse and diplomacy. Mexican officers, like cops throughout the world, are sensitive about protocol on their own turf, and any foreign police officer must remember that he's only in a position to request cooperation, not to give orders. An officer who enters Mexico and begins to behave like "big daddy" will cause his welcome to sour. One Los Angeles Police lieutenant didn't realize this when he went south of the border to handle a transaction that he would have been better off leaving to subordinates. When he became pushy, Mexican officers simply took the handcuffs off their prisoner and told the lieutenant he could do what he wished with him. The lieutenant stuffed the fugitive into the trunk of his car and made for the border without a police escort, leaving some physical evidence behind. Once on American soil, a charge of violation of civil rights by his prisoner became possible, and other officers had to get their stories straight to forestall such a move.[13]

Departmental Policies

During emotional moments in pursuit of their duties, police officers sometimes exceed their instructions, exceed departmental policies, and even infringe the penal code. One common type of incident relates to suspects who resist arrest, and who injure police officers in the process. Once in custody, it's "pay-back time." Either in the patrol car, or in the police station, the suspect may suffer injuries that will go on the report as having been incurred while "resisting arrest."

When several California officers beat Rodney King with their nightsticks on March 3, 1991, and an amateur videocamera operator caught it on tape, it was headline news for days. The trial, and the riots that took place in Los Angeles after the "not guilty" verdicts, kept the case in the headlines for over a year.

TV networks had originally released a carefully manicured version of the tape, edited to make the incident appear worse for the officers than it was. Indeed, this version of the tape played on national networks and local channels repeatedly, convincing many viewers that the officers were guilty without doubt. However, this was not the first such incident. In Kansas City, Missouri, police officers arrested James Sevart, Jr., after an hour-long pursuit. Sevart had fled when officers wanted to question him regarding a burglary. A local TV news crew video-taped the arrest, and the tape showed several officers holding Sevart down, while an officer struck him at least three times with an object and another officer kicked him.[14]

Even the Rodney King incident served a constructive purpose. While Los Angeles Police Chief Daryl F. Gates maintained that this was not typical, another police chief thought it important enough to use as training material. William Rathburn, a former LAPD Commander and the new Chief of the Dallas, Texas, Police Department, uses the videotape of the King beating as a training vehicle. His officers watch the tape and discuss the issues involved. Rathburn intends that no such incident will ever happen in Dallas.[15]

With all that, some officers continued to pummel civilians in front of video cameras. California Highway Patrolmen Reginald Redmond and Nicholas Chouprov received suspensions without pay for beating two Persian Gulf war protesters at an otherwise non-violent rally in January, 1991.[16]

In Huntsville, Alabama, a local TV station presented a videotape that allegedly showed a city police officer using excessive force on a suspect. The department suspended the officer with pay pending investigation.[17]

In Fort Worth, Texas, an officer who was videotaped beating a handcuffed suspect lost his job. However, a grand jury had knocked down assault charges against the officer, and the officer's lawyer said that he intends to appeal the department's action.[18]

At times, what first appears to be excessive force is justified. Police officers in Oregon shot a suspected drug dealer 28 times. The suspect had pointed an empty gun at them, but a grand jury ruled that the officers had no way of knowing the gun was empty, and that the shooting was justified.[19]

It's a mistake to use excessive force because of emotion, because such an incident can break an otherwise promising career. On the other hand, selective extra-legal application of force can serve good ends when lesser methods fail. This is what we call "curbstone justice."

Curbstone Justice: Short-cut Law Enforcement

This is summary punishment on the street, completely unofficial and without paperwork of any sort. After the incident is over, it's closed by mutual agreement. A police officer may administer a beating to a man disturbing the peace, instead of arresting and charging him. Some instances of "curbstone justice" cover more serious crimes. "Curbstone justice" or "street justice" is a traditional and time-honored method of informal law enforcement.

Often, cops hand out summary beatings to juveniles, perhaps compensating for the discipline they feel they did not get at home. One incident occurred shortly after World War I, when beat cops regularly worked foot patrol. A boy, riding as passenger in a stolen car, was stopped by the beat cop. This officer knew everyone in the neighborhood, including the boy and his family. Instead of arresting the boy, the beat cop slapped him hard across the buttocks with his nightstick and said, "Get the fuck outta here, ya little bastard, before I tell your father."[20] In this situation, the father's authority was more to be feared than the criminal justice system.

Several Philadelphia officers, after a report that a young girl had been molested by a suspect they knew, picked him up and brought him to the station. Several members of the squad pummeled him with nightsticks until he fouled himself, literally beating the shit out of him. They then took him downtown. The suspect did not file any charges against the officers, conceding that he'd gotten what he'd deserved.[21]

Sometimes curbstone justice serves as a deterrent when no other method, such as a restraining order, works effectively. One New York City detective of the pre-WWII era, "Broadway Johnny" Broderick, and his partner, Johnny Cordes, repeatedly got into altercations with suspects and became legends in their own time. A typical incident would begin as members of a "protection racket" gang tried to extort payments from a shopkeeper. A complaint to the police would bring about the arrest of the suspects, but later friends of the suspects would visit the shopkeeper and inform him that, if he pursued the complaint, he wouldn't live to testify at the trial. Broadway Johnny would confront the thugs who had made the threat and administer a beating, telling them that if they threatened the complainant again, he knew where to find them. This "hand talk" was much more effective than any injunction issued by a court. On the street, naked force gets suspects' attention much more than does a piece of paper.

A principle some officers follow is to dispense street justice to "rabbits," those who flee when ordered to stop. Quick administration of summary justice serves as a deterrent.[22]

At times, subtle methods of street justice serve to harass a lawbreaker. One method is to telephone a suspect's wife and tell her that her husband is having an affair. This method is more effective if a woman places the call. In other cases, planting physical evidence for the wife to find bolsters the accusation. A condom or women's panties on the back seat of the husband's car will convince all but the most trusting wife, and a phone call will ensure that she finds it.[23]

Some underworld figures obtain legitimate employment as a cover for their real activities. When this happens, one tactic is for an investigator to visit his employer and ask if the suspect works there, then leak that he's under investigation for organized-crime connections.[24]

Coping With Electronic Media

Police have always had problems with certain elements of the media. Inevitably, there are a few cop-haters who always interpret police actions in a negative light. If crime is on the rise, it's the fault of the police, even though the police are not the ones who commit the crimes. If police officers take any short-cuts in pursuing a case, these media people criticize them for using excessive force, or abuse of authority. Although it's obvious that you can't make an omelet without breaking eggs, police officers have to be magicians who can do exactly that, by their standards.

Conventional news reporting is dangerous enough when the reporter or his editor is a cop-hater. Electronic media can be worse, because video cameras can document a mis-statement by a police officer, using his own words or actions to fortify a media trial, convicting the officer on the six o'clock news.

The point for officers to note is that it's important to be very careful when using force, and to be mindful of the possibility that a camera may be recording the action. Using force outdoors or in any public place exposes the officer to the danger of an electronic witness recording his actions. The greater danger is that a news program director, in the race for higher ratings, may edit the tape to show the officer in the worst possible light, as happened in the Rodney King incident.

If it becomes necessary to use force on a suspect, an indoor setting is more secure because of limited access. Even a telephoto lens can't see through a wall.

The type of force is important, as well, because of visual impact. A videotape of an officer striking a suspect with a baton has tremendous visual and dramatic effect. This is true regardless of justification. A suspect who resists arrest and fights the officer can be made to appear as if he's merely defending himself against police brutality. By contrast, a shooting takes very little time, much less physical exertion, and doesn't appear as dramatic because there's less action.

Chemical agents are safe and effective. Overpowering a belligerent suspect with "Bodyguard" and similar aerosols is quick and not visually exciting. Obviously, there's no blood for color cameras to record, and although the suspect may feel as much physical pain from the effects of the pepper spray as from a baton, the scene doesn't appear as dramatic and sensational. This is very important for the officer working in an area where the media are hostile to police.

A valid justification for use of force is when the suspect assaults the officer. Of course, many suspects will submit to interrogation and search on the street, especially when outnumbered by police, and it becomes more difficult for the officer when there are witnesses or video cameras. There are, however, several ways of inconspicuously inducing a suspect to attack and justify the officer's use of force. One officer kept a pin in his Sam Browne belt, and would jab the suspect during a search. Another is to produce pain by jabbing the body's sensitive areas, such as the testicles or a tender spot in the armpit. Flicking a finger into someone's eye also will stimulate him to attack the officer. The officer blocks the view of witnesses by getting in close to the suspect. This works very well on a suspect driving a car, and it's possible to flick a finger quickly into his eye without passengers seeing it.[25]

The Ultimate Sanction: Execution

Summary execution of suspects is another topic on which sketchy information exists. Fictional cops such as Dirty Harry Callahan do it all the time, perhaps because Dirty Harry never has to face an officer-involved shooting investigation team, nor has to fill out the paperwork a killing requires. It's not an exaggeration to say that a shooting takes three seconds, and the subsequent paperwork takes three days.

Among cops, there's a lot of locker-room talk along the lines of "blow them away," the casually stated determination that the suspect's life is cheaper than dirt. Reality is different, because the consequences of an illegal shooting can be severe, involving both criminal and civil litigation.

As many officer-involved shootings take place in locales without witnesses, the only account of the events is the officer's. Without contradictory physical evidence, there's no way to dispute the officer's account. Planned street execution of a known criminal is a dangerous undertaking, but much easier for police than for private citizens because police know the subtleties of escaping detection. Leaving the scene after the execution is one way of avoiding official involvement.

The typical target for street execution is a very dangerous suspect, such as a cop-killer or organized-crime figure, who has frustrated previous efforts to obtain enough evidence to sustain prosecution. Organized-crime operators are especially difficult to prosecute because they're very street-smart and take precautions to use cut-outs who protect them from direct involvement.

There are several reasons for street executions of special suspects:

1. Execution can be in lieu of arrest and prosecution when solid evidence is unavailable.

2. Execution can prevent the suspect from continuing his criminal career and committing more crimes.
3. Execution can be an effective conclusion to a case that's inexpedient to prosecute even when enough evidence is available, such as one involving national security. One such instance, involving a double agent, was too awkward to prosecute, and violent termination was the best choice.[26]
4. Execution can serve as a deterrent, a warning to others in the same criminal enterprise. Execution is far more effective than a verbal warning to "Be out of town by sundown." The warning can be overt, such as the suspect's body left in a public place, or it can be more subtle, as in the case of a mysterious disappearance.
5. Finally, execution can be defensive. Some suspects are so dangerous that, if they threaten to "get" an officer or his family, it's imperative to take the threat seriously. Drug dealers, biker gang members, and a few others have assaulted and even killed police officers gratuitously, or for revenge. The shooting of Patrolman Byrne in Queens, New York, on February 26, 1988, was an execution with a head shot from a .38-caliber handgun. The killer had no substantial motive: he did it just for the thrill.

Execution of suspects can be "ad hoc" or systematic. A police officer holding a suspect may decide to "cancel his ticket" on the spot if no witnesses are present. Another way is a planned and informal action by two or more officers working together to ensure "back-up."

One peculiar incident of excessive zeal ended in death for a transient. The police chief of Clay, West Virginia, allegedly spiked wine bottles with castor oil in an effort to rid the town center of drunks. The chief had told others about his tactic of spiking wine, so that the word would spread to the winos and deter them from loitering in the center of town. One drunk, though, died of pneumonia three weeks after drinking wine allegedly spiked with castor oil. The Chief, facing an attempted murder charge, is free on bail, partly because he's the only law enforcement officer in town.[27]

Finally, there is the unofficial "special squad," operated in secret by a police agency. The Federal Bureau of Investigation did operate a totally secret squad apart from its regular roster, composed of agents who undertook special dirty jobs for the Bureau. These were completely unofficial, working outside normal Bureau channels.[28]

Organizing such a special squad requires special recruitment methods. A special squad operator is not a civil servant, and the squad does not place public advertisements for members. The process is always by word of mouth, with potential recruits available among military veterans, intelligence agency operatives, and even organized crime.

Paying a corps of extra-legal agents both salaries and expenses takes creative book-keeping. Police agencies have slush funds to cover expenses and payments to informers, designed to provide untraceable money. The FBI paid at least one unofficial executioner by falsifying his military records, listing him as a "wounded veteran," to provide him with a disability payment for the rest of his life.[29]

Tactical planning can be elaborate or simple. Police officers setting out to execute a suspect run the operation somewhat like a raid without the benefit of a search warrant. Goals are to accomplish the task and to avoid detection. Avoiding detection isn't as easy as it seems, because a badge isn't necessarily an asset. Many police agencies have their "Dudley Dorights," set upon furthering their careers by "burning" other officers, and encountering one of these can blow the plan sky-high and result in an indictment for murder.

The elements of a successful execution are:

- Proper identification of the target. Executing the wrong person is an intolerable error. Apart from taking an innocent life, a mistaken hit can cause an international incident. When Israeli hit men assassinated a Moroccan waiter they thought was a terrorist in Lillehammer, Norway, repercussions were severe.[30]
- Deciding upon a time and place where the target is unprotected or most vulnerable. This can be extremely difficult if the target has a large retinue and is always accompanied by bodyguards. Ordinarily, a simple ambush along the target's normal travel route or an attack at his home, will do the trick. In some cases, it's more desirable to set him up, luring

him to a certain place on a pretext, and disposing of him there or en route.

- Deciding on the method of termination. Firearms are the best choices, except in situations where noise precludes their use, or when it's desirable to make the death appear "accidental." Since most terminations are surprise assaults, the best way to assure results is firing multiple shots into the target. Depending on a single shot to the head or spine is too uncertain because people have survived such wounds. Firing a single fatal shot depends on good marksmanship, often in adverse conditions, such as darkness. This is especially true if the firearm is a handgun, because handguns are low-powered weapons, lacking the destructive power of rifles and shotguns. Power is sacrificed to make handguns light and concealable. Multiple shots, aimed at several vital areas, offer a better prospect of shutting down the body's systems quickly and permanently.
- Disposal of the corpse. In an overt execution, leaving the body for others to discover is relatively simple. If the target is a gang member, a ready assumption is that he was killed by rivals. In covert actions, it may be necessary to bury, cremate, or otherwise dispose of the cadaver. Burial can leave embarrassing remnants if the clandestine grave later becomes the site of a freeway or building. Another way is to have an arrangement with an undertaker, who can pack an extra corpse into a coffin. Once buried in the

cemetery, it's fairly certain not to be disinterred for many years.[31]

Handling and disposal of the corpse can be messy if the plan includes transportation to another location. As experienced police officers know, violent death is rarely neat or clean, and many targets vomit, or void their bladders and bowels as they die.[32] A body bag is a useful accessory to avoid soiling a vehicle during transportation.

Logistics for the execution can be simple and straight-forward. Obtaining a firearm or other weapon is routine for police officers because they often confiscate weapons from suspects and withholding an occasional one from the property office can build up a small supply of weapons not traceable to individual officers. If a firearm has previously been used in a crime, ballistic evidence can lead an investigation away from the officers involved.

Handguns are in demand because of their concealability, although an occasional termination plan requires a knife, wire, or rope. Unlike what happens in spy films, poisons rarely figure in terminations because they take too long to act and aren't as reliable or easily available as firearms.

Obtaining a vehicle for transportation to and from the execution site, or to carry the corpse, is easy for big-city officers with access to "laundered" vehicles. Undercover and narcotics units regularly have their vehicles re-registered with legitimate but untraceable plates, and an officer with a connection with such a unit can take advantage of the process.

Another way of terminating suspects is during a violent crime in progress. One police unit specialized in targeting repeat offenders. Unit officers would conduct surveillances while suspects were planning crimes and gathering weapons and other equipment. When the crime "came down," officers would act. The key was to interrupt the crime at the critical moment, making a gunfight inevitable. It was helpful if innocent lives were endangered by the suspects, because this would without doubt justify officers' use of deadly force.[33]

Most police problems aren't as dramatic as the extremes of suspect handling. More common is justifying search and seizure.

Notes:

1. *Law Enforcement News,* NY, John Jay College of Criminal Justice, October 31, 1990, p. 2.
2. *L.A. Secret Police,* Mike Rothmiller and Ivan G. Goldman, NY, Pocket Books, 1992, p. 37.
3. *Ibid.,* p. 41.
4. *Police,* July, 1992, p. 56.
5. *Family Of Spies,* Pete Earley, NY, Bantam Books, 1988, p. 327.
6. *S.W.A.T.* , December, 1989, p. 68.
7. *Law Enforcement News,* October 31, 1990, p. 4.
8. *City Police,* Jonathan Rubinstein, NY, Ballantine Books, 1973, pp. 32-233.
9. *Ibid.,* p. 204.

10. *L.A. Secret Police,* p. 93.
11. *The FBI-KGB War,* Robert J. Lamphere and Tom Shactman, NY, Berkley Books, 1987, pp. 208-209.
12. *L.A. Secret Police,* pp.180-181.
13. *Ibid.,* pp.181-183.
14. *Law Enforcement News,* October 31, 1990, p. 2.
15. *Law Enforcement News,* March 31, 1991, p. 2.
16. *Law Enforcement News,* June 15/30, 1991, p. 3.
17. *Law Enforcement News,* November 30, 1991, p. 2.
18. *Law Enforcement News,* November 30, 1991, p. 3.
19. *Law Enforcement News,* June 15/30, 1991, p. 3.
20. *City Police,* p. 190.
21. *Ibid.,* pp. 183-184.
22. *L.A. Secret Police,* pp. 34-35.
23. *Ibid.,* p. 91.
24. *Ibid.,* pp. 137-138.
25. *Ibid.,* pp. 38-39.
26. *The Squad,* Michael Milan, NY, Berkley Books, 1992, pp. 54-107.
27. *Law Enforcement News,* March 15, 1991, p. 4.
28. *The Squad,* pp. 3 & 6.
29. *Ibid.,* p. 47.
30. *By Way of Deception,* Victor Ostrovsky and Claire Hoy, NY, St. Martin's Paperbacks, 1991, p. 206.
31. *The Squad,* pp. 64-66.
32. *Ibid.,* pp. 105-106.
33. *L.A. Secret Police,* p. 124.

4
Search And Seizure

Searching suspects and seizing evidence have their own rules, established by statute and modified by case law and departmental policies. Officers must know the ins and outs of proper procedure to make a case stand up in court.

The need to secure evidence sometimes puts police officers in a dilemma. Basically, there must be "probable cause" or a search warrant to search premises, and failure of the officer to provide for one or the other results in the evidence's being suppressed in court. This is called the "fruit of the poisoned tree" doctrine. The purpose is to persuade police officers not to use illegal search and seizure, because they won't be able to introduce any seized material as evidence in court. However, there are ways to obtain evidence without the taint of illegality.

Dropping a Dime

This technique is to obtain probable cause to enter suspect premises. An investigating officer anonymously calls "911" to report that a "man with a gun" ran into the suspect premises. Another pretext is to report a fight or disturbance in progress. The police dispatcher sends a patrol unit, and when it arrives the investigators meet the uniformed officers. They announce that they just "happened" to be in the area, and offer to assist the patrol unit. Using this pretext, they enter the premises. Once inside, they can conduct a surreptitious search, plant evidence, etc.

Break and Enter

Another way to obtain probable cause is to break the door or window of the suspect premises, and have a patrol unit respond. This is especially easy to work if the premises are protected by an alarm service. The alarm company will call the police, or an automatic dialer and telephone tape will call "911." As before, investigators in the area offer their services to responding officers.

Previously Planted Evidence

Exploiting certain knowledge that contraband is on the suspect premises is easier in some areas than in others. While many judges will grant a search warrant upon an affidavit that "reliable information" has disclosed that there is contraband upon the premises in question, a judge's cooperation depends upon consistent results. The majority of search warrants have to produce evidence to maintain the officer's credibility and that of his "confidential sources."

There are right and wrong ways to plant evidence. As we'll see during the discussion of entrapment, there are ways of using informers to plant evidence for later discovery by a search team. A basic way to plant evidence is what we call the "black bag job," surreptitious entry.

Surreptitious entry is a standard technique of intelligence and counter-espionage agencies. Stealing confidential material from foreign consulates is one way of discovering another government's secrets. American intelligence agents did this routinely during World War II.[1] The Federal Bureau of Investigation had a special squad of unofficial agents who served the same function during much of the cold war.[2]

"Black bag jobs" are not monopolized by security police. Regular law enforcement agencies break and enter to obtain information and evidence when nothing else works. Mike Rothmiller, a Los Angeles investigator, pored over a suspect's telephone records and noted that his target had made many calls to a particular telephone in New York City. Obtaining the number's name and address from a cross-listing, he asked a contact of his in the New York City Police Department for information about that person.

When the New York detective contacted him shortly thereafter, he asked Rothmiller for a safe mailing address to which he could send some highly sensitive material. Rothmiller arranged with another police officer in another state to receive the package for him. The package duly arrived, containing address books, photographs, pieces of paper, and other material that had apparently been scooped up from someone's desk. The New York officers had broken into the target's premises and emptied out his desk drawers, sending the unfiltered material to Rothmiller for whatever he might make of it.[3] In this case, surreptitious entry served as a way to obtain evidence. It can also facilitate planting it.

Planting evidence can be simple or complicated, depending on the situation and the locale. One of the easiest ways is to drop a plastic envelope of marijuana through a partly open window onto a car seat. Many drivers, especially in hot climates, leave one or more windows open a crack to let hot air vent from the vehicle. A plainclothes agent can slip a "baggie" through the crack in a couple of seconds. The practical value of this technique is that many states have laws allowing police to seize any vehicle in which they find illegal drugs.

In some instances, other vehicles become the targets. Aircraft, much more expensive than cars, often serve to smuggle illegal drugs over the United States' Mexican border. Narcotics officers also use them for aerial surveillance. More than one aircraft has come into the hands of narcotics agents because an agent "happened" to be walking around the airport and noticed contraband on a seat.

Planting evidence in locked premises is much more difficult. This is almost always a team operation. The team leader decides what is to be planted, and where. He directs a surveillance team to stake out the premises to discover when the occupants have left. A reconnaissance team tries to discover what locks and other security systems are in use. Once there's enough information to determine whether or not entry is workable, the team leader makes the final decision.

If he decides that it's practical to get in and out without detection, he chooses his team for the operation. The outer perimeter will require a surveillance team equipped with radios or cellular phones to warn if any of the occupants are returning. A security team may be necessary to delay the return of the occupants if circumstances permit. One delaying tactic is staging a traffic accident. Another, more drastic method is to stage an altercation with the occupants, with either a fake drunk or mugger accosting them.

The entry team consists of an officer trained in picking locks without leaving evidence of forced entry, such as scratches or tool marks. His job is only to open and relock the locks without leaving traces. The "bagman" carries in the contraband and places it in a suitable spot.

Some premises, such as "rock houses," are too tough to enter. Rock houses are fortified drug dealers' premises, equipped with fences, guard dogs, booby-traps, and other methods of detecting and impeding entry. These are usually occupied 24 hours a day, making surreptitious entry impossible. In such cases, police officers have to find softer targets, such as dealers' residences, if they don't live in the rock house itself, or their vehicles. Planting contraband in a vehicle is a double-barreled tactic, because it deprives the suspect of transportation, thereby cramping his style, as well as providing an asset for investi-gators.

An officer searching a suspect can "discover" evidence on his person, in his vehicle, or in his premises. Some agencies label this as "proactive policing." An officer can help make an arrest "stick" by falsifying his report, such as claiming to have witnessed a criminal act when he only heard about it from someone else. Prosecution is cleaner and simpler if the officer states unequivocally that he witnessed the act.[4]

There are subtleties to committing perjury to reinforce a case. One is not to mention any facts which may help the defense. "I can't recall" is a common ploy to avoid disclosing something which may weaken the case.[5]

Handling witnesses who may buttress a suspect's defense is delicate, and one way is simply to leave them out of the report. Police know that overworked public defenders are unlikely to invest the time required to locate such witnesses.

When several officers are involved in an arrest, it's necessary to hold an informal conference to reconcile their statements, to assure that there exist no weaknesses or contradictions that may sabotage a case. It's often necessary to "doctor" arrest reports to simplify and strengthen the case, and officers must agree on the statements they'll provide in their reports and in court.[6]

"RICO" Statutes

During the last two decades, several laws at federal and state levels have come into being to hit harder at organized criminals. These are generally known as "RICO" (Racketeer Influenced and Corrupt Organizations) laws, and provide for summary confiscation of assets from criminals. RICO laws have become valuable enforcement and prosecution tools.

If a police officer walking by "happens" to notice a "baggie" on the seat of a sports car belonging to a narcotics suspect, he can seize the vehicle. With a paint job and a new set of license plates, the car is ready for use by undercover investigators, without straining the agency's budget. This provides incentive for investigators to plant evidence enabling them to seize vehicles.

Another important aspect is that seizing assets can hamper a suspect's defense. Confiscating a bank account or other liquid assets thereby makes prosecution easier because without the funds to pay a private attorney, the suspect has to rely on the public defender. Public defenders are typically inexperienced and overworked, with caseloads as heavy as those of police officers. A typical public defender is a recent law school graduate using the post to obtain experience before trying for a more lucrative job.

The typical public prosecutor comes from the same background as his counterparts in the public defender's office, and is no match for a tough and experienced trial lawyer. Affluent suspects who can afford to hire the best legal talent may never see the inside of state prison, stringing the case out with legal delaying tactics, until arresting officers and key witnesses have forgotten, moved away, or died. Even if convicted, they have a series of seemingly endless appeals to postpone serving the sentence. Depriving suspects of these options is a powerful weapon, which is why police officers and prosecutors alike welcomed the RICO laws.

Pitfalls in Serving Warrants

A search warrant affidavit is a legal document, and it's vital to get every detail right. Incredibly, some officers have compromised their cases and put themselves and their agencies in line for megabuck lawsuits by making simple errors, such as writing the wrong address on the affidavit. An innocent error can lead to charges of wrongdoing, even when the case is otherwise solid.

This has happened all over the country, with a variety of results. In Guadalupe, Arizona, police raided the wrong house because the case officer had not made a proper reconnaissance. In this instance, householders were very forgiving of the error. In another instance, federal drug agents broke the door of the wrong apartment, frightening the two young ladies inside. They apologized, repaired the door, and that ended the incident. However, in Kent, Washington, police served a search warrant at the wrong address in full view of a TV crew taping the popular program, *Cops.* TV crews captured footage of the husband and wife, and their four children, being dragged out of bed at gunpoint. The half-naked wife had her posterior recorded for posterity by the camera, although an officer later covered her. The problem arose because the wrong address was on the affidavit and warrant, and the case officers were not in the front line to show the raiding party the correct address next door. [7]

Taking short-cuts in law enforcement is risky, but as we've seen, a careless and innocent error can have serious consequences. The householder whose front door has been demolished by eager officers will be frightened and angry, and it's only a short trip to Jacoby & Myers.

Notes:

1. *Surreptitous Entry,* Willis George, Boulder, CO, Paladin Press, 1990, pp. 102-111.
2. *The Squad,* Michael Milan, NY, Berkley Books, 1992, p. 3.

3. *L.A. Secret Police,* Mike Rothmiller and Ivan G. Goldman, NY, Pocket Books, 1992, pp. 163-164.
4. *Ibid.,* pp. 31-32.
5. *Ibid.,* p. 31.
6. *Ibid.,* pp. 32-34.
7. Associated Press, May 25, 1992.

5
Informers And Information

A police officer's stock in trade is information, obtained from a variety of sources. Long before modern scientific investigation, police obtained information from people, as they still do today. People may be victims, witnesses, or associated with the suspect. The suspect's associates may be relatives, friends, employers, and others who have any dealings with him. These may include hotel clerks, prostitutes, co-conspirators, and others.

Police officers increasingly obtain information from inanimate sources, such as city directories and computers. We'll examine these carefully, because they're becoming increasingly important to investigators.

People

People who provide information to officers fall into two classes: *informants* and *informers.* Informants are those who have information that will enable police to find, apprehend, or convict the suspect, without being directly involved with his criminal activities.

Informants

Informants can be witnesses, passers-by, neighbors, and others. They may also be members or employees of private and public companies and departments. A contact in the Internal Revenue Service can disclose a lot about a suspect to investigators. One type of contact highly prized and used by police investigators is the former law officer working a security job with a private company. Many large corporations, such as credit reporting bureaus, hire former law officers as their security directors, and this network of former cops helps investigators obtain sensitive information without the formality of an official request or a court order.

Using such sources, investigators can obtain a suspect's telephone records, credit card records, bank records, and other privileged information. Former police officers who run their own private investigative agencies often have access to information outside normal police channels, and they cooperate when former colleagues ask for help.[1]

Informers

Informers are criminal associates, or people who inform for pay or other special consideration. Police and journalists often confuse these terms and use them interchangeably. Obtaining information from informants is fairly routine, requiring patience and good interviewing technique. Handling informers is another matter because informers always stand to gain from their relationship with the police, and indeed often initiate the contact in the hope of obtaining something for themselves. Informers often have criminal records themselves, and are not above fabricating information to sell for personal gain.

Informers' Motives

Informers operate from a variety of motives, all centering around personal gain, which need not be monetary. Drug dealers sometimes snitch on other dealers, using the police to suppress their competitors. An informer may "put the mouth" on a suspect for revenge. Yet another motive is to strike a "deal" with police or prosecutors, working for immunity or a reduced charge or leniency in their own problems with the law. Finally, there is payment, in money, drugs, or in simply being left alone to pursue criminal activities.

Officers sometimes allow prostitutes or professional gamblers to operate unmolested in return for a flow of information. Interrupting their business would result in breaking their contacts with the street, and information would dry up. It's expedient to allow relatively harmless offenders free rein to obtain information about heavy-duty suspects. This follows the principle of "trading up."

Handling Informers

Officers must always handle informers with a delicate touch, and keep them at arm's length. Informers have been known to "work both sides of the street." The snitch may be feeding false information to officers for money, or to falsely accuse someone else in return for their freedom. Another prospect is the double agent passing false information to officers to ingratiate himself with the suspect, or to save his life, because sometimes the penalty for snitching is death.

At 7 A.M. one summer morning in Phoenix, Arizona, federal agents raided an apartment occupied by a parolee who purportedly was dealing drugs. After the lead agent opened the door with his battering ram, agents rushed in to be nauseated by an overpowering odor of putrefaction. One agent thought that the apartment contained a corpse. Agents opened the windows, turned on the air conditioner, to air out the premises. During the search, they found chicken parts in the garbage can, but no drugs. Belatedly, they realized that the occupant had not been home all weekend, and suspected that he had left the chicken parts in a hot apartment for their benefit, as a practical joke. [2]

A basic principle in handling informers is always to insist on "trading up," as we've seen. The informer must always give better than he gets, or it isn't a profitable deal for the officer or prosecutor. There's no percentage in letting a burglar go to arrest a jaywalker.

Informers are notoriously venal, and it's no exaggeration to say that some would even sell their mothers. They'll also sell out the control officer, which is why officers handling informers must always guard against lies, using the carrot and the stick. The "carrot" is payment for information, which works well with some trustworthy informers who value both money and the officer's esteem. This "positive reinforcement" is not enough with others.

For difficult cases it's always smart to keep the "stick" in reserve. Experienced officers know that having a "twist," or threat, to use against an informer who plays dirty is often the only way to keep him in line. A "twist" may be the threat of sending the informer back to prison, or threatening to leak the news that he's passing information to the cops, which can lead to a death sentence from his underworld buddies.[3]

Cross-checking informers' statements is necessary because of their propensity to fabricate information to please the control officer and collect payment. If possible, the officer should have two informers, both unknown to each other, providing information on the same target. If the information doesn't reconcile, the officer knows that something is wrong.

Cross-checking can become very elaborate, especially when another agency becomes involved. Agencies trade informers and information, but they don't always play fair with each other. One agency may hold back information, or pass on bad information, because rivalry and territoriality still exist in police work. This is especially true when federal agencies deal with local ones.

In one case, a police investigator learned that a former "mob" member had moved into his area. The local FBI office was using him as an informer because he'd already provided evidence in a case against the mob and was under the protection of the Federal Witness Protection Program. FBI agents reasoned that the former mobster had local mob contacts and would be able to provide information regarding their activities.

The police investigator interviewed the mobster, who told him that he wasn't telling the FBI much of value, because FBI agents were easy to fool. He told the officer that providing the FBI with good information would expose him to danger, now that he was trying to keep a low profile and begin a new life. The FBI was paying him $1,500 per month for his bogus information. The police investigator compared the information he obtained from this informer with what the FBI said he had told them. The local investigator was suspicious that the FBI wasn't sharing all of the information they'd obtained. Later, the investigator told FBI agents that their informer wasn't spilling all he knew, but they didn't take him seriously because of their boundless self-confidence.[4]

Crossing The Line

Informers sometimes cross the line into another category, the "agent provocateur." This is an instigator who leads his associates into committing an act for which they can be arrested and indicted. We'll study case histories of instigators in later chapters.

Using Computers

As we've seen, computers can be very useful in finding local fugitives. Tapping into utility company computers is common, but finding suspects who are long gone requires wider and more imaginative use of modern databases.

A "database" is a computerized collection of information, such as a suspect's name, address, drivers license number, social security number, numbers of his credit cards, etc. Using such databases enables tracing someone literally across the country.

Some of the databases that help trace people are: credit reporting company records, airline reservation computers, Social Security Administration files, Internal Revenue Service computers, welfare computers, and bank computers. Bank computers can be especially useful because they can provide almost hourly locations of people who use credit or debit cards habitually.

These databases are in common use by private investigators, who often gain access to data files in total secrecy.[5] An example is tracing missing spouses in civil actions.[6]

Law enforcement agencies find computer tracing very useful, especially in today's climate of mobile and sophisticated lawbreakers. The FBI's NCIC, accessible by practically all law enforcement agencies in the country, has proved its worth in over two decades of operation. The Internal Revenue Service uses computerized matching to compare declared incomes against lifestyle databases to find those who are living beyond their officially declared incomes.[7] This is easy to do, because comparing credit card purchases and automobile registrations against individuals' Form 1040s discloses those who claim modest incomes, yet own expensive cars and charge opulent vacations.

FinCEN (Financial Crimes Enforcement Network), for example, enables tracing money launderers trying to "lose" illegally-gotten assets.[8] Gathering information about money movements and generating profiles of the individuals concerned enables building up an accurate picture of illicit financial transactions and the people who perpetrate them.

TECS II (Treasury Enforcement Communications System, Version II) is a computerized "watch list," a database of undesirables useful to customs agents and other police forces at ports of entry. This allows checking everyone who tries to enter the United States against a master list of possible suspects. Port of entry checking goes beyond identifying criminals. This is also useful for government security agents trying to identify foreign agents trying to enter the United States.

The United States is not the only country with computerized watch lists at ports of entry, as this is common practice throughout the world as a basic frontier security measure. Early detection of foreign agents and their couriers allows tracing them within the country from the first moment, and this can lead to uncovering their contacts and associates.

Persistent investigators need not worry about various restrictions placed on the dissemination of privileged information. As we've seen, the network of former police officers cooperates in extracting privileged information from restricted databases.

Fortunately for law enforcement, various "privacy acts" exempt law enforcement agencies from limitations placed upon privately-operated information-gathering services. However, this may change, perhaps because of abuses and breakdown of security. The General Accounting Office found that TECS II has its problems. There was a high percentage of errors, which could lead to effort wasted in investigating innocent people, and one suspended employee of TECS II was illicitly gaining access to the database.[9] This leads to the need for greater security.

Information Security

A basic principle in operating any law enforcement intelligence operation or network is secrecy. One reason is to prevent the bad guys from knowing how law enforcement officers may track them, and therefore devising countermeasures. Another reason has to do with public reaction. Large-scale information gathering necessarily spreads an electronic dragnet that includes a majority of people innocent of any crime, just as a drunk driver roadblock inconveniences and delays many perfectly sober motorists. This creates a ready-made issue for civil libertarians, a necessary evil in a free society.

The public remains necessarily unaware of thousands of well-conducted and successfully concluded investigations aided by computer tracking of suspects. However, one abuse or mistake can lead to serious consequences as injured innocent parties are manipulated by self-seeking lawyers and politicians. Attorneys, of course, enjoy a major lawsuit against the government, because they're almost guaranteed excellent remuneration for their efforts. Politicians, especially those with minority constituencies, have a ready-made campaign issue when they can posture against "racism." That a computer cannot be bigoted is irrelevant to politicians, who find championing minority causes a ticket to certain re-election.

This is why all law enforcement activities involving computer databases must remain top-secret. It's important to assign only the most trustworthy officers to such duties, officers who have proven themselves and their integrity in other sensitive assignments. Some agencies with secret investigative units impose a Mafia-like secrecy on their activities.[10]

There are many methods of maintaining and enforcing secrecy of paper and electronic intelligence files. A basic way is to keep them off police premises. Officers' homes, and privately rented storage facilities serve the purpose, ensuring that no unauthorized police personnel will accidentally discover them. In one case, detectives transferred a triplicate file to a public storage locker, which a detective had rented in his own name and paid for with cash taken from a slush fund.[11]

Another reason for private storage of files is to put them beyond the reach of organizations such as the American Civil Liberties Union and court orders. It's impossible to subpoena material if you don't know it exists, or where it may be.[12] Today, sensitive files take up little space when stored on high-density computer disks. The ease of duplicating disks ensures that vital files need never be lost, even if a politically-minded chief decides to disband the unit.

It's also important not to allow any information about these projects to become public knowledge, under any circumstances. An enterprising journalist, given a glimpse into the massive amounts of data on individuals available to law enforcement agencies, can generate an immense amount of publicity that can kick back against the agencies concerned.[13]

Gathering information is an important step towards clearing the case. After arrest comes a process that can save valuable time if it works. This is obtaining the suspect's confession.

Notes:

1. *L.A. Secret Police,* Mike Rothmiller and Ivan G. Goldman, NY, Pocket Books, 1992, pp. 165-166.
2. The author witnessed this incident.
3. *L.A. Secret Police,* p. 93.
4. *Ibid.,* pp. 135-136.
5. *Privacy For Sale,* Jeffrey Rothfeder, NY, Simon & Schuster, 1992, pp. 63-88.
6. *Ibid.,* pp. 106-112.
7. *Ibid.,* p. 142.
8. *Ibid.,* pp. 136-137.
9. *Ibid.,* pp. 138-139.
10. *L.A. Secret Police,* p. 21.
11. *Ibid.,* p. 9.
12. *Ibid.,* p. 19.
13. *Ibid.,* p. 23.

6
Obtaining Confessions

Once a suspect is in custody, police and prosecutors combine efforts to obtain confessions, for several reasons. The evidence leading to the arrest may be weak, and a confession wraps up the case and makes conviction almost a sure thing. Another reason is that a confession makes a lengthy trial unnecessary, thereby saving on police, prosecutorial, and court costs. With suspects too poor to pay their own lawyers, the state saves on the cost of a court-appointed lawyer. Confession is often a prelude to a plea-bargain.

Some suspects decide to tough it out because they're ignorant of the nature of the evidence. Once a defense attorney gets into the picture, he may advise the suspect to plead guilty to a lesser charge, or in return for a lighter sentence.

The basic rule here is that the earlier a defendant confesses or pleads guilty, the better deal he's likely to receive. If he decides to fink on his companions before police file charges with the prosecutor's office, he may avoid prosecution altogether. In some cases, the suspect may be able to obtain immunity by "trading up," which means providing information on someone suspected of a more serious crime, even if the object of his disclosures is unconnected with the present charge.

Emotions, Confession, and Irrational Decisions

Emotions can play a major role in obtaining confessions. Suspects often act against their best interests because of the effect of overpowering emotion. Guilt, for example, plays a major role with situational offenders such as the hit and run driver. A minister arrested for molesting children will almost certainly feel acute embarrassment and guilt, and the investigating officer can use these feelings to elicit a confession.

At times, simply telling a suspect that he'll "feel better" if he gets it off his chest will persuade him to confess. The officer carefully leads the discussion away from how the suspect will feel while he's spending several years in prison. The officer's appeal is to emotion, not logic. This is the principle behind sympathy ploys and other emotional tricks.

Sympathy ploys don't work well with the habitual offender and street-smart suspect. He's not vulnerable to appeals that he'll "feel better if he gets it off his chest" and other nonsense. With this type of suspect, it's better to appeal directly to his self-interest, using "deals," falsified evidence, and intimidation.

Investigators are also vulnerable to emotion, and sometimes make irrational decisions. This is most likely in high-profile cases in which they receive a lot of "pressure" to make a case. The investigator swayed by emotion instead of logic can go into an interrogation convinced that the suspect is guilty, and obtain a confession, despite the lack of corroborating evidence.

With enough intensive effort during interrogation, many innocent people will confess. Officers tempted to speed the process by coaching their subject unwittingly pass investigative keys to him, then listen to the subject feed them back during his confession.

One noted instance was the Wylie-Hofert murder in New York City, during the early 1960s. Two young ladies in their early 20s were sodomized and killed, and because one victim was the niece of Phillip Wylie, the novelist, pressure on the police was intense. Her father, Max Wylie, although not as famous as his brother, had important connections. Police arrested a young man and interrogated him, and his confession contained important investigative keys, such as the role of a jar of Noxema in the rapes. It later developed that the confessed suspect had an unbreakable alibi, and police had to release him.

More recently, nine people were murdered at Wat Promkunaram, a Buddhist temple just west of Phoenix, Arizona, in August, 1991. This mass murder immediately developed international complications, with the Thai Government concerned with its solution. Maricopa County Sheriff's investigators received a phone call from an inmate of a Tucson psychiatric hospital, stating that he and several others had committed the murders. Sheriff's officers, desperate for a break in the case, took the psychiatric patient's statements at face value, and arrested him and three others. They confessed after intensive interrogation, and sheriff's officers conducted a fruitless search along the freeway between Phoenix and Tucson looking for evidence allegedly discarded as the suspects drove back to Tucson. The suspects later retracted their confessions, stating that they had been coerced.

In November, 1991, Air Police at Luke Air Force Base stopped a youth and discovered a firearm which turned out to have been the murder weapon in his vehicle. This development, supported by physical evidence, forced a re-evaluation of the case against the first suspects. Eventually, two young men living in the Phoenix area were charged with the crimes. Sheriff's officers had to release the original suspects. Three of the original suspects have filed suit against the Maricopa County Sheriff's Office.[1]

Miranda

The "Miranda" Decision, delivered by the U.S. Supreme Court almost three decades ago, established that police officers must advise suspects of their rights when they take them into custody. The key word is "custody." No Miranda Warning is necessary during the early stages of an investigation. This greatly helps the investigator because suspects may still think that by appearing cooperative, they'll deflect suspicion from themselves. A suspect confident that he can "talk his way out of it" leaves himself vulnerable to low-key interrogation until the moment the officer has enough evidence to make the arrest. Of course, the private detective or security officer does not have to give a Miranda Warning, because the Bill of Rights was designed to protect citizens only from the government, not from other citizens.

Today, police agencies issue officers Miranda Cards, giving the form of the warning. Some agencies issue bilingual cards, with "Miranda" in both English and Spanish. Others have a space for the suspect to sign at the bottom, to acknowledge that he did receive the Miranda Warning. Although tradition-minded officers curse the Miranda Decision, saying that it makes their work harder, there are many ways to obtain confessions from suspects, and police still manage to keep the jails full.

Circumventing Miranda

American police officers have developed several ways to lessen the effect of Miranda upon interrogations. While they still read the suspect his rights, to conform to the judicial requirement, they sometimes deliver the warning in an offhand manner, implying that it's only a formality.[2] Another way is to avoid giving the warning, but stating that they did if the matter comes up in court. This is perjury, but in many cases judges and juries will believe the officer over the suspect.[3]

Immediate Confession

Suspects are often emotionally most vulnerable upon arrest. This is why it's important to make a maximum effort to isolate and disorient them once the handcuffs are on. A store security officer (private security officers are not obligated to "Mirandize" suspects) will bring the suspect to a back office, away from familiar places and faces. Police station interrogation rooms are always hidden away, preferably without windows, to remove the suspect from anything familiar and comforting.

It's at this emotionally most vulnerable moment that police and security officers can press for an immediate confession, sometimes by exaggerating the charges. Telling the suspect that he's the one responsible for a string of robberies or auto thefts can bring the admission that he only carried out one or two.

Interrogation Ploys

There are many tricks and techniques of interrogation, developed by hard-working police officers over many years of experience. Most fall into one of several classifications. There are "hard-line" approaches, and several varieties of softer methods. Officers use deception with a clear conscience, knowing that most suspects lie to them, anyway. Pretending sympathy, blaming the victim, and other emotionally dishonest tactics are normal in manipulating suspects into confessions. Sympathy is likely to work with the situational or first-time offender, such as an employee who stole company property, but with street-wise career criminals, it's necessary to take a stronger line. Emotional or physical brutality are the only languages they understand.

"Let's Make a Deal"

Any street-smart suspect knows his rights, whether the officer advises him or not. Suspects watch TV cop shows too. Theoretically, hardened career criminals should not say a word to the arresting officer, and demand to see an attorney immediately. In real life, it's not that simple. In fact, some suspects are eager to make a deal.

Police and suspects alike know that there rarely is honor among thieves, and that one will sell out another to secure an advantage for himself. In some cases, there's a race between arrested suspects to cut a deal that will result in a lighter sentence, even if it means testifying against a partner in crime. Some will even place all of the blame upon their partners in an effort to convince officers that they played only minor roles in the crimes. There are several techniques officers can use to improve their chances of persuading a suspect to make a deal.

Divide and Conquer

Playing one suspect against another is a favorite technique that takes advantage of criminals' distrust of each other. It's necessary to keep arrested suspects separate, so that they cannot compare notes. This allows the interrogator to mislead the suspects and manipulate their minds.

"Your Buddy Confessed"

Telling one suspect that his partner has confessed is a trick to use against a suspect who's not too bright. Truly street-smart suspects understand that confession is a race between contenders, and that after one has confessed and made the prosecution's case, officials don't need confessions from the others. This is a stupid way of playing one off against the other, but it still works at times. The only benefit for police and prosecutors is to simplify prosecution and save on court time.

A variation on this trick is to separate a pair of suspects, then bring one to the interrogation room for a period of time. It's not necessary to actually speak with the suspect, just to give his partner the impression that he's being interrogated. When the officer brings the suspect back to his cell, he thanks him for his cooperation within earshot of the other and promises to try to "do something" for him. He then takes the other suspect in for interrogation, letting him worry about what his partner confessed to the officers.[4]

A variation on this technique is to leave one of the suspects in an outer office while questioning his partner. After awhile, the officer calls out to his secretary to come in to take a statement. After a period of time, the officer leads the partner back to his cell and brings the other suspect in for questioning. The time spent wondering what his partner said softens up the suspect, making him amenable to a deal.[5]

Graymail

Not all suspects seeking to deal roll over and play dead. At times, their position allows them to be very aggressive and demanding, and deal negotiation then becomes a two-way street because police and prosecutors don't hold all the cards. This happens when the suspect uses "graymail."

"Graymail" is the art of threatening to reveal very damaging information at the trial if the prosecutor insists on pursuing the case. At times, corruption reaches so high in a police agency or its parent government body that there's intense pressure to abandon prosecution and let sleeping dogs lie. An example is the house of prostitution patronized by judges and politicians, which enjoys relative immunity. When "the fix is in," police must tread carefully.

Another example comes when the suspect's activities can open a can of worms if revealed. One case that came to light was the prosecution of a person identified only as "Jim" who was arrested for attempting to bribe an Internal Revenue Service clerk for taxpayer information. "Jim" was an underground trafficker in computerized information, culling it from credit bureaus, and a variety of legal and illegal sources.

The background to this case is that there is an underground industry furnishing supposedly private information about individuals to private investigators, credit bureaus, and other parties who pay the fees. Some of this information comes through strictly illegal means, such as purloining telephone company records for unlisted numbers, and private investigators posing as medical personnel to raid hospital records. Bribing government employees to hand over restricted documents is another illicit method, but it's very successful and widespread because it's strictly sub rosa.

The clerk accepted Jim's offer and immediately reported the incident to superiors. The IRS investigated, and soon Jim was under indictment for trying to blackmail a federal employee and for dealing in illegal information. However, Jim had a ready countermove, because during his career he'd amassed information about the rich and famous, such as Sylvester Stallone, General Richard Secord, boxer Michael Spinks, and other notables. He threatened to bring this information out in court, causing scandals, and this brought the prosecutor to heel.

The result was that Jim obtained a sweetheart deal, instead of a long and harsh prison sentence. He was not to do anything illegal for a year, and for six months operated as an informer for the

IRS and FBI, helping them with investigations of other information-gathering agencies involved in culling data from restricted government files. The icing on the cake was that Jim was actively helping federal law officers to shut down his competitors, as well as being able to pursue his own business almost unmolested.[6]

Sympathy

Pretending to sympathize with the suspect to make him or her open up is worthwhile, especially when the suspect is not a street-smart and hardened criminal. The purpose of sympathy ploys is to relax the suspect by making his crime appear less significant than it is, so that he feels more comfortable discussing it with the interrogator. This can be very effective with a person accused of assault during a domestic dispute, for example. The interrogator who sympathizes with the suspect, admitting that he's been tempted at times to use force on his wife, improves his chances of eliciting a voluntary confession.

"Everyone Does It"

The investigator attempts to dilute the emotional charge of guilt and shame by sharing the guilt. An example might be shoplifting or employee theft. The police officer takes advantage of the common knowledge that many people steal small items, especially from employers.[7]

The "everyone does it" technique leads into another ploy, "salami-slicing." This is cajoling a confession from the suspect in installments instead of one dramatic breakthrough. The officer begins by suggesting that the suspect surely must have thought of taking something at one time or another. With this critical first admission, the next step is to suggest that he may have stolen something insignificant, then something of more value. Step by step, the suspect admits to greater and greater misappropriations until he confesses the crime in question.

Blame the Victim

This is a crude attempt to mitigate or erase the suspect's guilt by shifting the blame onto the victim. Again, in a case of employee theft, the officer states that the employer is cheap and exploits his hired help, thereby justifying the theft. In cases of date rape, the officer takes advantage of the common knowledge that some women practice sexual teasing, and he gives the suspect absolution for having raped his date.[8]

Blame Society

This variation on the theme of absolving the suspect from guilt is effective because it takes advantage of the fashionable belief that "society" is somehow at fault for individual transgressions. Some suspects have a self-pitying attitude that sets them up for this ploy, and the interrogator can use this as an opening to elicit a confession. Feigning sympathy for the suspect by recognizing that he's had a hard life resulting from a broken home, ghetto upbringing, etc., can give the impression that the interrogator is on his side, after all.

Flattery

Another way of playing on a suspect's emotions is by flattering him on the skill he showed in his crime. Praising his skill as a fraud artist, safecracker, or burglar can pump up his ego so that he's more willing to describe exactly how he did it.[9]

Psychological Ploys

At times, investigators have a suspect, but no evidence. In other cases, they have solid information, but from an informer they wish to keep in his undercover role. This rules out having the informer testify in court. Then it becomes necessary to use psychological trickery to obtain evidence and a confession. Publicized instances of these methods include FBI agents' interrogations of espionage suspects.

Ronald Pelton was a National Security Agency employee who allegedly had sold cryptographic information to the Soviets. The FBI had only the word of a defector who had since redefected to the Soviet Union, and a tape of a wiretap on the Soviet Embassy, made in 1980. On this tape, Pelton spoke in very guarded language about "something I would like to discuss with you I think that would be very interesting to you." This was worthless as evidence, because it was so vague. However, FBI agents reasoned that it might work as a psychological lever to pry Pelton's lips open.

In November, 1985, FBI agents rented rooms in the Annapolis Hilton to provide a neutral setting, and one agent telephoned Pelton, asking him to come to the hotel to discuss a matter of "extreme urgency." Three agents took chairs in an arc around Pelton's chair, so that Pelton would have to turn his head to speak to one or another. One agent told Pelton that he was going to tell him a story, and asked him to keep silent until he'd finished. The agent then began a tale about a young man from Pelton's home town, and told how he had followed a career in the Air Force and the NSA, and finally phoned the Soviet Embassy to offer to sell classified information. The agent obviously tailored the story to resemble what he thought Pelton had done. He then played the wiretap tapes, then asked Pelton to finish the story.

Pelton wasn't biting yet, and he replied that the story, while interesting, did not describe him. When the agent replied that it was Pelton's voice on the tape, Pelton countered by stating correctly that the tape did not make a case.

The agents continued the mind game, teasing Pelton with vague hints about "cooperation," trying to imply without actually committing themselves that they wanted him as a double agent. When Pelton stated that he'd want to consult an attorney before committing himself to helping the FBI, the agents replied that having an attorney present would only complicate the situation because security needs would mandate that the attorney would have to be cleared first. This was on the thin edge of legality, because if Pelton had stated clearly that he wanted to speak with an attorney right then, the agents would have been obligated to discontinue the interrogation.

Now was the time for equivocation and a little deception, using ambiguous language that hinted, but did not state, that Pelton would not be prosecuted if he cooperated. An agent pointed out that "...many cases involving national security just do not result in prosecution."

Pelton fell into the agents' trap, believing that they had more evidence against him, and convincing himself that the government would not prosecute if he opened up and revealed everything. After answering many more questions, the agents kept up the charade by telling him that he was free to go meet his girlfriend. Actually, agents kept a close tail on him and at 9:30 that evening, an agent telephoned Pelton to tell him that they urgently needed to meet with him at the hotel. Pelton, having had a few drinks and a narcotic bought on the black market by his girlfriend, was relaxed and his guard was down. Agents counted on fatigue dulling Pelton's mental processes enough so that they could prod him into revealing incriminating information.

Under questioning, Pelton revealed where and when he'd met his Soviet contacts, and provided more details. Then came the question that agents felt was vital to making a case that would stand up in court. An agent asked him if he had been aware that turning over such information to the Soviets would harm the United States. Pelton, after some equivocation, admitted that he knew that passing the classified information to the

Soviets would harm American interests. Soon after, an agent "Mirandized" and arrested him.[10]

FBI agents used a similar mixture of hints and bluffs to cajole another espionage suspect into confessing. This was Larry Wu-Tai Chin, a Chinese-born former employee of a CIA subsidiary. Chin had begun working for the United States in 1948 as a translator for the U.S. Army Liaison Office in Foochow, China. He moved up to the U.S. Consulate in Shanghai, and ended up with the CIA's Foreign Broadcast Information Service. This service keeps watch on foreign media.

Although Chin was not cleared for classified information and his nominal job description did not give him access to classified information, he worked hard and earned the confidence of his superiors. Informally, he gained access to secret material because CIA personnel often needed documents translated, and they cut red tape to do it. Chin obtained American citizenship and a security clearance, and continued to pass secrets to the Red Chinese until he retired from the CIA in 1981.

FBI agents used a similar psychological approach to conceal their cards, because they'd obtained information from a double agent they wished to protect. An agent told Chin stories about two hypothetical people, one of whom cooperated with the FBI, and the other who did not.

Chin hoped to avoid prosecution and bit down on the hook, suggesting that he'd be interested in becoming a double agent. FBI agents told him that he'd first have to divulge everything he knew. Holding out the hope of immunity, they milked him dry, then arrested him. His trial resulted in conviction, based mainly on material he'd provided.[11]

Psychological ploys can be very effective against suspects who are not street-smart, and who are vulnerable to bluff. Bringing a white-collar suspect into a room with surveillance photographs of himself adorning the walls can convince him that officers have been watching his every move, and already know everything. This is intimidating, and provides the setting for a variant of the tricks used on Pelton and Chin.

"We already know all about what you did. What we need is information about your conspirators. Help us with that and we can make a deal." This offer, with the implication of immunity, can pry open the lips of the guilty but naive suspect.

Deception

At times, sticking strictly to the facts doesn't have enough effect, and it's time to try something stronger. With criminal suspects, it's morally correct to deceive, by implication, mis-statement, or omission, to obtain cooperation. It's also correct to appeal to the suspect's need for a favorable outcome, turning this into self-delusion. This is the basis of the first technique:

Dropping The Charges

Persuading a suspect that charges against him will be dropped if he confesses may appear incredible to the reader, but to a suspect under severe emotional tension it can be made realistic. This depends upon two points: that the crime not be too serious, and that it's up to another person, rather than the law, to press the case. For example, a suspect accused of theft might be willing to believe an interrogator who tells him that, if he confesses, he'll have his employer drop the charges. Once the detective has the confession, he sends the suspect back to his cell. He can always explain later that the employer did not agree to drop the charges. Even if the suspect later realizes the deceit, and that the officer reneged, what can he do?

This can also work when the investigator needs information about another case or suspect, and can persuade the suspect that the prosecutor will consider dropping the charges in return for cooperation. It won't work if the investigator has to put it in writing, which will almost inevitably be so if the suspect has his attorney with him.

A variation on this theme is the "Can you take it back?" ploy. The officer implies that if the thief returns the stolen property the victim will drop the charges. The officer must be careful not to make a direct commitment, or put anything in writing.[12] Obviously, this sort of arrangement won't pass if the suspect's attorney is present.

The Fake File

Using a fake or phantom file can serve to undermine any of the suspect's statements that an officer cannot challenge directly. This trick requires a prop, a file folder, with a few sheets of paper inside. When the suspect makes a statement the officer considers questionable, he can simply open the file, pretend to read for a few seconds, and reply, "That's not what it says here."[13]

Overcoming objections and challenges from the suspect is just as easy, because the officer simply uses the authoritarian approach. If the suspect asks what it says in the file, the officer can simply reply, "You're not asking the questions here. I am!"

The Phantom Charge

One way of prying a confession to a certain crime from a suspect is to convince him that he's under suspicion for something far worse. A suspected burglar can be told that he's under suspicion for a murder committed on the street next to the site of the burglary. A variant is to ask the burglar to explain the corpse found on the premises after he left, making it appear as if he'd murdered someone during the crime. Yet another variation is to exaggerate the amount of a theft or robbery. In all these cases, the suspect may take the opportunity to "trade down," confess to a lesser crime to avoid being charged with a more serious one.[14]

Minimizing The Charges

This is almost the reverse of the phantom charge, and some suspects lead themselves right into this set-up. A suspect eager to deal may not only sell out his partner, but try to inflate his partner's importance and minimize his own role in the crime. Pretending to accept the suspect's statement as absolutely correct in every detail helps make the breakthrough to obtain the confession. Even with its distortions, the confession works as a lever in breaking the rest of the case. Faced with a partner's confession, especially if it's exaggerated and places most of the blame on him, a suspect may retaliate and confess the crime as it really happened. The prosecutor can resolve any discrepancies during the trial, and indeed use the contradictions to impeach the suspects' credibility.

The Accident

Another way of minimizing the charges is to suggest that the deed was the result of an accident or mistake of some sort. This works especially well if the suspect has already begun to rationalize his role in his own mind. Some suspects, desperate for a way out, grasp at any straw to deny or minimize their guilt, leaving the way open for the officer who knows how to exploit the opportunity. The suspect may be ready for the rationalization that he didn't really mean to steal something, but merely slipped it into his pocket and was later reluctant to disclose it because he feared being accused. In more serious cases, the officer may agree that the gun went off accidentally during a robbery that left the victim dead, for example. This is not the time to bring up the "felony murder" law, which states that any death during the commission of a felony leaves the perpetrator charged with first-degree murder, whatever the circumstances.[15]

"Let's Finish This and Go Home"

This is another outright deception that takes advantage of a suspect's yearning to put an end to his ordeal and be released from custody. It works best at the end of the workday or late at night, when the suspect is tired and not as mentally sharp as he was earlier. The interrogator tells the suspect: "Look, let's get this over with. I know you're tired. I'm tired too. Let's wrap it up so we can all go home." A suggestible suspect may accept the simplistic and naive proposition that confessing will bring him his freedom.

Intimidation

When softer approaches don't work, officers may try intimidation. There are many ways of intimidating suspects without using physical force. Sometimes, the mere suggestion of physical force can create anxiety in a suspect, which the cop can exploit. One or more husky, mean-looking cops can put fear into a suspect, without making any explicit threats.

The Mind Game

One way of intimidating the suspect is setting the scene for a mind game. Those who are not professional criminals, but white-collar criminals or occasional offenders are not sophisticated, and are vulnerable to this sort of intimidation. As previously discussed, candid photos of the suspect in various settings mounted on the wall, for example, suggest round-the-clock surveillance.

"Innocent People Have Nothing to Hide"

This is a powerful technique that will work with all but the most case-hardened, street-wise suspects. Telling the suspect who wants to remain silent that innocent people have nothing to hide deprives him of the refuge of silence by making it clear that his very silence is an indicator of guilt. Logically, this suggests that the person is guilty until proven innocent, but the interrogator relies upon emotion, not logic, to win his case.

The interrogator can use this after delivering the Miranda Warning. Telling the suspect that he has the right to remain silent, but if he does, it's an indicator of guilt, can pry his lips open.[16]

The Suspect's Family

Intimidating a suspect by using subtle threats against his family can pry a confession from him, but only if it's clear that police actions will remain strictly within the law. Otherwise, working his family against him can backfire and break careers.

One way to do this is to emphasize how difficult it will be for the suspect's wife to cope with interrogation, if she's also a suspect. If not, pointing out how hard the trial will be on his family can be persuasive. Only by confessing himself can the suspect save his wife and family this ordeal. Another approach is to point out the hardships that his family will suffer as a result of his imprisonment. Suggesting that his children will be subject to torment by classmates as a result of publicity puts the loyal family man on the horns of a dilemma. The alternative is to confess, make a deal, and receive probation instead of prison.

With a suspect who is not too bright, or fairly suggestible, it's possible to stretch this technique to outrageous lengths. The officer can tell him, "If you work with us now, your wife need not ever know about this." Alternatively, he can promise that the suspect's mother, neighbors, or other associates won't find out about his difficulties if he cooperates now. This defies logic, but it works with a few suspects.

Good Cop/Bad Cop

Another form of intimidation is to use the good cop/bad cop technique, also known as the "Mutt and Jeff" technique. This is the whipsaw approach, using both sympathy and threats, with one interrogator snarling and acting in a menacing manner, while his partner is sympathetic and conciliatory. The alternating "hot and cold" treatment breaks down a suspect's emotional resolve, and the surprising aspect is that this works, even on persons who know the trick, because it hits at gut level, not upper cortex. Detectives investigating the killing of a female motorist by a California Highway Patrolman used the good guy/bad guy technique against their suspect, Patrolman Craig Peyer.[17]

Tape Recordings

Some police investigators routinely tape record interrogations, both to ensure having an accurate record, and to be able to confront the suspect with his own words later. Tape recordings are valuable for intimidation, and they stand up in court.

Experienced investigators know that people who have just faced life-threatening incidents are emotionally aroused, sometimes not quite in control of themselves, and they may make statements that can later work against them. Recording a statement while a suspect is emotionally distraught can be very valuable, especially if incriminating.

Investigators don't always record statements, however. An example is a police officer who just shot and killed a robbery suspect. He may say something like; "When I saw that nigger pull his gun, I shot him." Investigators know that, if they record such a statement, or write it down verbatim, this can serve as justification for a wrongful death lawsuit, a peg upon which a civil rights group can hang a propaganda campaign, etc. Therefore, they do not tape record an officer's initial statement, only a sanitized version, and they go over his statement carefully with him before making their report. They do not extend such courtesy to civilians involved in shootings, even though the circumstances may be very similar.

Taping a Miranda Warning helps establish that the officers actually warned the suspect according to law. However, there are ways to fake it. Leaving blank tape at the beginning of an interrogation allows inserting the Miranda Warning later. Clumsy officers, or those unsure of themselves, sometimes repeat Miranda Warnings to their detriment. Repeating it several times can alert even the stupidest suspects and induce them to shut up for their own good. Therefore, it's sometimes desirable to omit the warning, or delay it, until the suspect has made enough damaging admissions.

The "Plant"

A common way of obtaining information is using a "plant" in a prison cell. A cellmate can be an undercover officer, or a police informer. Even a genuine felon awaiting trial or serving time after conviction may be seeking material to trade for a "deal." One such was William Plew, whose testimony regarding a prison confession was important in the prosecution's case against Ruben Melendez, accused of stabbing another inmate to death in 1987. The complication came because Melendez sought help from a "jailhouse lawyer," allowed under Arizona Department of Correction rules. He chose Plew, who assisted him and later obtained parole for himself. Later, after his arrest for passing bad checks, he offered to "make a deal." Authorities had him slated as a key witness in Melendez' trial, but the issue of confidentiality obstructed the prosecution. The defense stated that, as Plew was acting as Melendez' attorney, the lawyer-client confidentiality principle applied, and Plew would not be allowed to testify.

Further complicating the issue was Plew's not being a licensed attorney, merely a jailhouse lawyer.[18]

This case illustrates the basic principle on covert information-gathering. An informer may provide valuable information to police and prosecutors, but even if the information is conclusive, bringing it into court is another matter. The dubious status of informers can make practical use of their testimony difficult or impossible.

Recently a case went up to the U.S. Supreme Court and established that an informer cellmate can provide testimony at a trial, circumventing the need for a Miranda Warning. This was Arizona v. Fulminante, Supreme Court No. 89-839. This cellmate, however, was not a jailhouse lawyer.

The conviction against Oreste C. Fulminante had previously been reversed in the Arizona Supreme Court, Case No. CR-86-0053-AP, on the grounds that "admission of defendant's involuntary confession was a reversible error," because the government informer had used implied threats to coerce the confession. The suspect had been convicted of killing his eleven-year-old stepdaughter, Jeneane Michelle Hunt, by shooting her twice in the head with a large caliber weapon at close range. At the time, police did not file charges, as the evidence was insufficient and contradictory, and Fulminante left the state.

Later, while Fulminante was serving time in a federal prison for an unrelated charge, he made damaging admissions to another inmate. Upon his release, the same inmate and his fiancee picked up Fulminante at a bus terminal, and Fulminante stated that he could not return to Arizona because he had killed a little girl there. Police arrested him and returned him to Arizona for trial.

His appeal was based on the informer's telling him that he was in danger of physical harm from other inmates. Many inmates do not like "baby killers" and at times will assassinate them in prison. The informer told Fulminante that if he confessed to him, he would protect him from other inmates. The Supreme Court held that the confession was admissible, especially because Fulminante had confirmed it to the informer's fiancee upon his release, in circumstances which certainly were not threatening. The bottom line was that a "harmless error" did not call for automatic reversal of a conviction in this and other cases, a result of the Chapman v. California (1967) case.

Polygraph Examination

The polygraph, or "lie detector," isn't as reliable as its proponents claim, a fact which is becoming widely recognized in the law enforcement community. The polygraph measures only some physical symptoms of stress, none of which correlate reliably with truthfulness or mendacity. One of the original developers of the polygraph, John Larson, conducted a controlled experiment with the polygraph to test its reliability. He found it to be hopelessly inaccurate, and denounced polygraph testing as a "racket."[19] Further evaluation by the Office of Technology Assessment of the United States Congress found serious faults with it.[20] This is why criminal courts have disallowed use of polygraph "evidence" during the 70-plus years since the device appeared.

Even when investigators use the polygraph only as an investigative aid to determine a person's truthfulness, results can be contradictory. One aspect of its use in the recent Mesa, Arizona, Police Department sex scandal investigation shows this clearly. A major controversy was whether or not Mesa's Assistant Chief, Del Ballentyne, acted properly in pursuing the investigation after being told of widespread officer misconduct by an officer's wife. Cherie Staton, the wife of Officer Russ Staton, who was discharged and later convicted of child molestation, claimed that she had told Chief Ballentyne about other officers' sex escapades in 1988. Ballentyne countered with the statement that he did not recall Staton's making any such allegations to him. Cherie Staton took a polygraph test in 1992, and passed. Ballentyne at first refused, but then submitted to the test, and the polygraph showed him truthful, as well. This turned out to be a classic case of "What did he know and when did he know it?" but the polygraph proved to be no help at all in clearing up the question.[21]

From this, it's clear that the polygraph is as unreliable today as it was during its early developmental years. Nevertheless, the polygraph is still a valuable investigative tool. This is because the crafty investigator uses it as an intimidation tool, taking advantage of suspects' credulousness and suggestibility. The polygraph technician makes every effort to convince the suspect that "the instrument will not be beaten," and thereby persuade him to admit the truth.[22]

Some polygraph technicians literally stack the deck against their subjects, asking them to pick a card from a deck in which all cards are the same, then informing them that the machine has "detected" their deception.[23] The purpose of tricks such as these is to convince the testee, without actually putting it into words, that the machine is infallible. Other technicians will make the blanket statement that the machine is never wrong. This works to bluff some people, who when they find out that they'll be asked to confirm their statements while hooked up to a "lie detector," break down and confess before the session begins.

Some suggestible people will react positively to the testing itself, with the needles going almost off the chart because the suspect has been led to believe that his stress level will increase if he lies. This allows the technician to draw a clear opinion that the suspect was deceptive, and confront him with it after the test. However, even if the chart tracings are unclear and equivocal, they can still serve to intimidate the suspect during the post-test interrogation.

The post-test interrogation is equally important because it provides a third opportunity to break the suspect. The technician goes over some of the questions with the suspect, never stating outright that the suspect lied, by pointing out that there is a "problem" with some of his responses. This puts the burden of clearing himself on the suspect, making it harder for him to deny complicity. The critical point about the post-test interrogation is that the technician can use the results against the suspect whether the charts show any objective indication of deception or not.

In a criminal investigation using the polygraph, it's important to work with a sophisticated polygraph technician who understands the realities of the situation and who will co-operate with the investigator. The purpose of a polygraph test is to extract a confession or a damaging admission. By itself, it's not admissible in court, but if it can pry a suspect's mouth open and lead him to disclose damaging evidence that the investigator can verify independently, it can help "make" a case. An example is the murder suspect who breaks down under polygraph testing, and who admits the crime and tells the investigator where he hid the weapon.

There's really no moral objection to using the polygraph as an interrogation tool. The genuinely innocent person is in no danger, because the results can't serve as evidence in court to convict him wrongfully. The suggestible guilty person is open to suggestion, and the polygraph can induce him to confess.

In some cases, a stupid or very suggestible person is open to outright deception. In one case, which has become a legend in its own time, investigators placed wires from a photocopy machine on a suspect's arms. When the suspect gave an answer they didn't like, an officer pushed a button on the machine, and out came a sheet of paper with "He's lying" on it. This story, which has been attributed to several police agencies in different parts of the country over the years, may be only legend.

The only serious problem is the street-smart suspect who understands his rights, and knows that police cannot force him to submit to a polygraph test. The investigator is thwarted at the outset, and will have to find another method of obtaining the material he needs for his case.

Torture

Another type of coercion is physical torture during interrogation. Slaps and punches are common forms of physical coercion, but sometimes torture takes exotic forms. In 1985 a sergeant and a patrolman at New York City's 106th Precinct used a stun gun on several suspects to induce confessions.[24] They were convicted and sentenced to prison. As previously noted, this incident resulted in a lawsuit against the city. Another officer was cleared of charges after six years of delays.[25]

Stun guns are useful for "curbstone justice" and as interrogation tools, provided officers use them properly. The mistake officers have made in the past is not realizing that stun guns tend to leave characteristic first-degree burn marks on the skin. Pairs of marks spaced the same distance as stun gun electrodes result when applying the stun gun through clothing, because the high-voltage current arcs and burns the skin.

Applying the electrodes directly to exposed skin greatly reduces the possibility of burns because of the direct contact. A further step is wetting the skin first, preferably with salt water. Best of all is conductive jelly, used for electrocardiograms and for electro-shock treatments, obtainable at a medical supply house. Improvising conductive jelly by mixing saturated salt solution with vegetable lubricant, such as "K-Y," is another way to prevent burns.

Whatever the means, it always helps to elicit a confession. At times, however, a suspect doesn't make it into the police station. This is allowable if the suspect's demise doesn't involve the officer in a disciplinary proceeding or a criminal charge. At times, however, there is a mistaken shooting which can shatter a career. Taking an innocent life is bad enough. Being prosecuted, with its severe effects on the officer's family, is worse. This is why we'll examine alibi guns next.

Notes:

1. *Arizona Republic,* August 5, 1992.
2. *The Mugging,* Morton Hunt, NY, Signet Books, 1972, pp. 121-122.
3. *Ibid.,* p. 127.
4. I*nterrogation: Techniques of the Royal Canadian Mounted Police,* Anonymous, Boulder, CO, Paladin Press, 1991, pp. 47-48.
5. *Ibid.,* p. 49.
6. *Privacy For Sale,* Jeffrey Rothfeder, NY, Simon & Schuster, 1992, pp. 86-88.

7. *Interrogation: Techniques of the Royal Canadian Mounted Police,* p. 12.
8. *Ibid.,* pp. 13-15.
9. *Ibid.,* pp. 42-43.
10. *Merchants of Treason,* Thomas B. Allen & Norman Polmar, NY, Delacorte Press, 1988, pp. 205-215.
11. *Ibid.,* pp. 298-303.
12. *Interrogation: Techniques of the Royal Canadian Mounted Police,* p. 55.
13. *Ibid.,* p. 30.
14. *Ibid.,* p. 37.
15. *Ibid.,* pp. 52-54.
16. *Interrogation,* Burt Rapp, Port Townsend, WA, Loompanics Unlimited, 1987, p. 70.
17. *Badge of Betrayal,* Joe Cantlupe & Lisa Petrillo, NY, Avon Books, 1991, pp. 73-85.
18. Associated Press, January 14, 1991.
19. *A Tremor in the Blood,* David Thoreson Lykken, NY, McGraw-Hill, 1981, p. 30.
20. *Ibid.,* pp. 55-62.
21. *Maricopa County Attorney's Office Investigative Report, Mesa Police Department Internal Affairs Complaint No. 92-24 and 92-53.* Prepared by Paul W. Ahler, Deputy Maricopa County Attorney, Chief, Special Crimes Division.
22. *Lie Detection Manual,* Dr. Harold Feldman, NJ, Allison Press, 1982, p. 28.
23. *Ibid.,* p. 161.
24. *Police Marksman,* July/August, 1985, p. 24.
25. *Law Enforcement News,* NY, John Jay College of Criminal Justice, June 15/30, 1991, p. 2.

7
Alibi Guns: Uses And Abuses

Another area of rule-bending is the "alibi gun," or "throw-down knife," used to justify a mistaken shooting. The alibi gun should be untraceable to the officer, of course, which precludes his dropping his back-up gun at the scene. Some officers, when they confiscate a weapon from a suspect they do not arrest, keep the weapon for themselves because they know that it can serve to justify an arrest or a shooting in certain circumstances.[1]

It's easy for an officer to obtain an alibi gun by confiscating it from a suspect. Often, a street-smart suspect understands the officer's motives, but also understands that it's in his best interest to play along to avoid criminal charges.

An officer who obtains an alibi gun may be causing complications for himself if the gun's previously been used in a crime. Some suspects aren't too dismayed by losing their guns to an acquisitive police officer because this provides a one-way gate for losing the evidence. If the officer is later discovered to have the gun by his superiors, he can't point the finger at the suspect from whom he confiscated it because this would implicate him in an illegal cover-up.

The same danger exists when buying a firearm from an illegal source or from a casual acquaintance. It isn't easy to trace a gun's provenance without making official waves, and a gun with a record can be incriminating in its own right. If it's on a list of stolen property, mere possession can bring serious consequences.

William Jordan, a former U.S. Border Patrolman, describes the rationale behind the alibi gun in his book, *No Second Place Winner.*[2] Jordan relates a hypothetical case of a person who matches a suspect's description, and who reaches in his pocket for a handkerchief after being challenged by an officer. The officer, thinking that the person's reaching for a weapon, blows him away. It's worth noting that he wrote this book after he'd retired. It would be unwise for any police officer to endorse the use of an alibi gun while still serving, as his words might return to haunt him in court one day.

New York's Harlem riots of 1964 began when a police officer shot a Black youth, stating that the youth had attacked him with a knife. There was a knife on the scene, but some residents alleged that the officer had thrown the knife down after shooting the suspect. A police investigation cleared the officer, but this did not satisfy critics, who felt that the investigation had been a whitewash.

Many police agencies make it somewhat difficult for an officer to carry an alibi gun. The rules state that any firearm carried by a police officer must be department approved, inspected, and registered. If an officer wants to carry a "back-up" gun, for extra protection in case his weapon malfunctions or is taken by a suspect, he must submit it for inspection by the departmental armorer, and must "qualify" with it. "Qualifying" means that he must demonstrate his proficiency with it on the firing range.

This still doesn't stop the officer from carrying an alibi gun. It merely prevents his using his back-up weapon to alibi a wrongful or mistaken shooting. Most police officers carry patrol cases with them to hold the forms, statute books, extra handcuffs, and other paraphernalia they need on patrol. The patrol case is normally beside them, on the front seat of the car. Inside can be a small handgun wrapped in a rag or plastic bag, in case of need.

What's not obvious to people, except police officers, jurists, and lawyers, is that a firearm isn't necessary to justify a shooting. A knife will do as well at close ranges. This includes distances out to 21 feet. Since most police-felon shootings take place at close ranges, a knife or club will serve as an alibi weapon.

Another misconception is that the alibi weapon must be clean of the officer's fingerprints. Not necessarily. Normal police practice is to remove any weapon from a suspect's hand, even if he's down and apparently incapacitated. This is a prudent safeguard against a suspect's reviving and resuming his aggression. A pistol or knife may well have the officer's fingerprints on the outside. The only caution the officer must observe when preparing an alibi gun is not to have his prints on the ammunition. In fact, it's not even necessary to have the handgun loaded, because the officer is not obligated to spot a suspect the first shot in an affray.

Notes:

1. *City Police,* Jonathan Rubinstein, NY, Ballantine Books, 1973, p. 289.
2. *No Second Place Winner,* William Jordan, privately printed, 1965, pp. 15-17.

8
Obtaining Evidence

There are several classes of evidence that can help or make a case. Verbal evidence is statements from victims, witnesses, and suspects. Documentary evidence is paperwork, such as forged checks, that help establish guilt. Physical evidence takes in fingerprints, fired bullets, tire tracks, and other types of tangible evidence of crime.

Experienced investigators value physical evidence because they know that it increases the chances of clearing and prosecuting a case.[1]

Physical evidence is so valuable that, as we'll see, officers sometimes generate it themselves.

Wiretapping

Wiretapping, bugging of premises, and other electronic surveillance techniques have had their ups and downs. They've been legal at times, totally illegal after some court decisions, and legal with a warrant in other jurisdictions.

Police officers sometimes use illegal methods in conducting investigations. Officials of the Missouri Highway Patrol placed illegal wiretaps in internal investigations during the 1980s. Col. C. E. Fisher, Missouri Highway Patrol Superintendent, called the wiretaps a "stupid" way to obtain information.[2]

Wearing A Wire

A "wire" is a slang term for a microphone or recording device hidden on the person. There are several varieties, all battery-operated, and their purposes range from monitoring a deal for the undercover officer's protection to securing and recording damaging admissions for prosecution.

A simple radio mike transmits to a nearby receiver and/or recorder. A tape recorder does not transmit, but records for as long as the tape cassette lasts. The microphone, which is necessary for both transmitter and recorder, has to be where it will pick up sound with minimal interference. It may be disguised as a tie clip, button, etc., but it cannot be concealed under clothing. Clothing masks and muffles sound, and its rustling generates interference which can overpower the sound to be recorded.

The transmitter or recorder can be almost anywhere. Two favorite places are in the small of the back, and in the groin area. Because of cultural sensitivities to searching the groin area, this is fairly safe, but not against someone who knows the trick and orders a strip search. Wearing a wire has become almost ineffective against experienced organized-crime figures because they're both sophisticated and cautious. If they have the slightest suspicion, or feel that they don't know their co-conspirator well enough, they'll insist on a full body search before getting down to business.

Undercover officers using recorders behave in a certain way, asking the target to be very explicit in his statements, and to recite or repeat the obvious. This can tip off the subject that he's being maneuvered into making damaging admissions.

Countermeasures used by street-smart criminals to avoid having their conversations recorded and used against them include:

- Caution in discussing sensitive topics with casual acquaintances.
- A full search of anyone who might be wearing a recorder or transmitter. It's important to note that wire-wearers favor the small of the back and the crotch.
- Discretion while using the telephone. This is standard practice among organized crime

leaders, who always assume that any line may be bugged.

- Never holding any sensitive discussion in the other person's premises or car, which might have a well-concealed bugging device.
- Insisting that any meeting or discussion of sensitive topics be moved from the originally planned location, because of the possibility that the premises may contain bugs. Even public places can be dangerous this way, because of "shotgun mikes" and other listening devices.

Notes:

1. *Forensic Evidence and the Police, The Effects of Scientific Evidence on Criminal Investigations,* National Institute of Justice Report, 1984, pp. 69-70.
2. *Law Enforcement News,* NY, John Jay College of Criminal Justice, December 15, 1991, p. 5.

9
Manipulating Evidence

Physical evidence is the strongest way to "make" a case. At times, physical evidence you may need simply isn't available, and it's necessary to fudge to obtain a conviction or confession. In other instances, the evidence is solid, but it's necessary to shade the truth regarding its acquisition. This is, strictly speaking, perjury, but it happens every day.

Perjury has two main uses; to justify an affidavit for a search warrant, and to supply "probable cause." Police officers often use information obtained from snitches in their warrant affidavits. Often, this information is impossible to check out before making the affidavit, but the officer will perjure himself and state that he did check it carefully.[1]

Occasionally, this practice kicks back at the officer. A Boston, Massachusetts, detective received a sentence of five years on probation for inventing a fake informant in a warrant affidavit. During the raid, the convicted officer's partner was shot to death. A consequence of the fudging of the affidavit was that much of the evidence that would have served in convicting the suspect who shot the officer was thrown out.[2]

It's common to fudge testimony to establish probable cause, thereby justifying an otherwise illicit search. An officer who takes a drug user out of his car and finds a baggie of marijuana in the glove compartment or under the seat will testify that he smelled marijuana smoke, or saw a few marijuana seeds on the front seat.

Police frustration at not being able to make good cases against people they know are guilty sometimes spills over into illicit acts. Planting evidence is one act that frustrated investigators use. This goes by various names, depending on the locale. It's called "farming" in Philadelphia, and "flaking" in New York.

The morality of planting evidence is as clear as its illegality. The simple fact is that most crimes do not result in clearance, and habitual offenders "get away with it" until they are apprehended. Investigators who know that a suspect is guilty may have no moral problem with helping their case along with illicit means.

It's one thing to "frame" an innocent person, and another to construct a case against someone with many prior arrests and convictions. Experienced investigators use two rules of thumb to form snap judgments of guilt or innocence.

The first relates to past behavior. A person with a record of theft convictions is more likely to be guilty than someone with no "priors." The other takes in immediate circumstances, including opportunity and motive.

Any officer who plants evidence risks his career, and even his freedom. The Chief of San Juan Bautista, California, was convicted of conspiracy and falsifying evidence on July 14, 1990. This related to a 1988 case in which he added marijuana to a quantity of seized drugs so that he could increase the charge from a misdemeanor to a felony.[3]

Sheriff's officers in Maricopa County, Arizona, raided a suspect's home seeking illegal drugs. The officers planted a marijuana bush in the suspect's yard while other deputies were interrogating him inside. Then they brought him out to see it, in an effort to make him think they had solid evidence against him.

On September 19, 1985, Maricopa County Sheriff's officers conducted a raid on the home of Billy Roy Brogdon, alleged to have been cultivating marijuana in his home. Officers planted marijuana plants on a tilled patch on Brogdon's property, then brought him out to see it in an effort to make him confess. This particular effort failed, because Brogdon was never prosecuted, and later unsuccessfully sued the sheriff and his deputies.[4] As we'll see later, it would have been better for the officers to have had an informer or agent-provocateur working for them plant the marijuana to provide them deniability.

Fingerprints

Many people, including some police officers, still believe the myth that it's impossible to fabricate fingerprint evidence. Not so. The modern photocopy machine makes it easy, because it uses fine powder, known as "toner," to reproduce the image. The toner clings to the image on an electrostatic drum, and a heating element fuses the toner to the paper. The trick is to place a suspect's fingerprint card on the platen and make a copy of it, but with the heater disconnected. This leaves a non-fused image on the paper copy, and it's possible to "lift" one of the non-fused fingerprint images with tape.

Obtaining Contraband

Obtaining material for use as "evidence" isn't very difficult. In many busts, it's possible to divert a quantity of drugs or other material for later use. Some police officers, especially narcotics officers, do not turn in all the material they encounter. Some reserve a small stash to use to pay informers. Some states, for example, now have laws allowing officers to preserve only a small sample of illicit material while destroying the rest, if the amount is too large and unwieldy to transport and store until the trial. An officer can withhold enough to serve as a supply for other purposes. The rationale is that if an informer is addicted, it's better to pay him with confiscated drugs than to give him taxpayers' dollars with which he'll patronize the illicit drug trade. Secreting a private stash of drugs is highly illegal, and paying an informer in this currency is also against the law, but it often happens.

The officer doing this is usually on his own, and his agency will disown and discipline him if it comes to light. A Phoenix, Arizona, officer was suspended without pay for 40 hours for conducting illegal searches and paying informers with drugs. The fall-out from this case was the resignation of two other officers and dismissal of a third. These officers set up drug buys, then allowed their snitches to keep the drugs as payment.[5]

Evidence and Leads

Illegally obtained evidence is not admissible. However, inadmissibility doesn't preclude its usefulness. A break-in can provide leads to where it's possible to obtain evidence legally. Working a "deal" with a suspect, and even interrogation without reading his rights, can produce information useful to the investigation.

An important point for experienced investigators to understand is that even a weak case with planted evidence can still result in jail time for the offender. Many accept plea-bargains to avoid the risk of a longer sentence resulting from a conviction after trial.[6]

This is most common with street criminals who can't afford private attorneys. Over-worked public defenders, knowing that practically all of their clients are guilty as charged, anyway, typically advise them to take a plea. Full-scale trials consume time, and this is the only way public defenders can cope with their heavy case-loads.

Notes:

1. *City Police,* Jonathan Rubinstein, NY, Ballantine Books, 1973, pp. 386-394.
2. *Law Enforcement News,* NY, John Jay College of Criminal Justice, June 15/30, 1991, p. 2.
3. *Law Enforcement News,* July/August 1990, p. 3.
4. *Tempe Daily News/Tribune,* February 25, 1988.
5. *Arizona Republic,* October 20, 1990.
6. *Under Cover: Police Surveillance in America,* Gary T. Marx, Berkeley, CA, University of California Press, 1988, pp. 153.

10
Entrapment

"Entrapment" is inducing an otherwise law-abiding citizen to become involved in crime. Although laws vary from state to state, there are general guidelines that distinguish a legitimate undercover operation from entrapment. First, the suspect must have demonstrated a predisposition to commit the crime. A record of convictions for the particular offense is good documentation of this principle. Another point is that the suspect must have repeated the act several times, to show a pattern rather than a single impulsive or random act. Witnesses can be crucial, and having the suspect commit his crime in front of others helps buttress the case. Finally, the undercover officer must not take part in the crime. Keeping his hands clean is crucial to his credibility.[1]

Police "stings" often border on entrapment, and sometimes they clearly cross the line. One such case, conducted by the Maricopa County, Arizona, Sheriff's Office several years ago, shows this clearly.

Two unemployed truckers answered a classified ad. The person who placed the ad, an undercover sheriff's officer, had advertised for a trucker to move a cargo to Texas. The officer met with the truckers in a diner, where he explained that the load was marijuana, and discussed the logistics and fee with them. They agreed to take on the job, and one evening met the officer at a warehouse in Mesa, Arizona, to load the cargo. Just before the truckers reached the freeway on-ramp, sheriff's cars stopped them, and officers made the arrest. The county attorney declined to prosecute, because of the questionable nature of the case, but the two truckers had an arrest on their records.

One type of sting is using an undercover officer to pose as a killer for hire, and to arrest the suspect when he makes the offer. This works because some people are so eager, or so foolish, in going about hiring a contract killer, that they disclose their intentions to casual acquaintances, who in turn inform police. An undercover officer poses as a "killer for hire," and makes the arrest once he obtains the suspect's voice on a hidden tape recorder, or obtains payment for the projected killing.

Another type of sting is to use an informer to entrap the target. Entrapment is illegal, and if a police officer is the one who conducts the entrapment, it can destroy the case. This is what happened with the two truckers. However, if a third party, working for the police but unknown to the prosecutor and defense attorney, can make the set-up, his role can be so low-profile that he's out of the picture when the arrest comes down and when the case goes to trial. A simple example is the informer who agrees to plant drugs in the target's home or car. In the simplest method of operation, he lays a baggie of marijuana on the seat of the car. Later, an officer walking by just happens to see it lying in plain sight, and this provides probable cause for search and seizure. Alternatively, an officer can stop the car when the target is driving it, and "happen" to see the baggie, giving him cause for an arrest.

The informer can also serve as agent provocateur, someone who induces a person to commit a crime. The informer, not being a police officer himself, need not appear in any official records. He can, however, persuade a target to commit a crime where the police are waiting for him. Officers can relate the incident in a way that makes it appear that they just "happened" to be on the scene when the suspect committed his crime.

One such was the FBI informer who joined "Earth First!", an ecological movement based in Tucson, Arizona. Members admired Edward

Abbey, author of *The Monkey Wrench Gang,* a novel advocating and describing physical destruction of equipment used by corporations despoiling the environment. The FBI agent provocateur persuaded members of "Earth First!" to destroy power lines leading to a nearby nuclear generating plant, and FBI agents were waiting for them.

One successful case of entrapment of a person without a previous record was that of a Florida businessman seeking money to reorganize his football team. A man telephoned him, offering to set him up with investors who would supply the money. A condition of the deal, according to the agent provocateur, was that the businessman supply the investors with cocaine. At first, the businessman refused, but later relented and introduced the agent provocateur to two men who sold him cocaine. This resulted in a conviction and prison term for the target of the investigation.[2]

Delivering illicit materials to the target of an investigation is another way to use an informer and agent provocateur. Los Angeles officers seeking to make a case against anti-war activists arranged for their agent provocateur to deliver a case of hand grenades to their home. This led to their subsequent arrest for possession of the grenades.[3]

Undercover operations also border on entrapment, and often cross the line because they offer many opportunities for officers to "set up" a suspect. This type of set-up is very flexible, versatile, and safe to conduct because of the tenuous nature of the link between an informer and his control officer.

An informer/agent provocateur can play a role in planting evidence. The informer can emplace the contraband before arresting officers arrive, to provide the officers with deniability in case of an investigation. Only the leader of the raiding party need know that planted evidence is waiting for discovery.

The important point is to have the informer sign an agreement in which he understands that he is not to break any laws during his service as an informer. The control officer explains to the informer that this is merely a formality, which it is, and that in practice the informer will have a free hand to use whatever methods, legal or illegal, that he and the officer decide to use. The paper only comes into play in case something goes wrong, and the informer's link to the police comes to light. Having this document protects the officer from complicity, as it shows that the informer was operating on his own, without authorization.

At times, law officers conduct entrapment by mail-order, and they have made their cases stick. During the late 1980s, the U.S. Postal Inspectors conducted "Operation Looking Glass," directed against child pornographers. In 1986, law officers raided a Los Angeles film company and secured a list of customers for pornographic films and videotapes. Postal inspectors set up an operation with a mailing address outside the United States, and sent advertisements to people on the film company's customer list. One man they arrested was Kenneth J. Hendin, of Sarasota, Florida, on a charge of receiving two videotapes of teen-age and pre-teen boys engaged in explicit sexual activity.[4]

Some of the cases built up by postal inspectors have been questionable. One postal inspector corresponded with clients, adopting the sobriquet of "Richard Teninch." He succeeded in enticing a Phoenix man into describing his child molestation exploits, under the guise of soliciting manuscripts for publication in a kiddie-porn anthology.

It's easier to work a sting on obviously criminal enterprises, such as car theft rings. One such operation took place as a cooperative effort between state and federal authorities in New York and New Jersey. Undercover officers bought cars from this ring, which employed professional car thieves who stole vehicles to order. Officers requested late-model luxury cars, which the rings stole and delivered to a warehouse in Carlstadt, New Jersey, which FBI technicians had equipped with hidden video cameras.[5]

A very successful "sting" was the notorious "AZSCAM" Project, which netted several state legislators who accepted bribes from one Joseph Stedino, working for the Maricopa County, Arizona Attorney's Office under the name of "J. Anthony Vincent." Vincent-Stedino passed himself off as a high-living mob personage, and his original task was to insinuate himself into illegal gambling circles in Phoenix. Soon, however, he learned that several state legislators were amenable to selling their votes. Introduced by an intermediary, Stedino approached legislators and propositioned them in rooms bugged by law officers. He suggested that affluent gambling interests wanted Arizona to legalize casino gambling, and were willing to pay for votes. This resulted in several of them accepting bribes on-camera. Some of these legislators resigned, and some stood trial. Several have served prison time for their offenses.

What was remarkable about the AZSCAM sting was that Stedino was able to play his game for as long as he did. He operated for many months before one legislator he'd approached alerted police. None of the others, even those who had declined his offer, had reported him to police, suggesting that there exists a tolerance of bribery among Arizona legislators. It also suggests that many legislators who were not themselves open to bribery were reluctant to turn in their colleagues who were doing wrong.

Notes:

1. *Undercover Work,* Burt Rapp, Port Townsend, WA, Loompanics Unlimited, 1986, p. 42.
2. *Under Cover: Police Surveillance in America,* Gary T. Marx, Berkeley, CA, University of California Press, 1988, p. 130.
3. *Ibid.*, p. 134
4. *Tampa Tribune,* April 13, 1988.
5. *Newark Star-Ledger,* January 11, 1992.

11
Pro-Active Enforcement

"Pro-active" policing is in sharp contrast to "reactive" law enforcement. Most police officers are reactive because they respond when a crime is in progress or has been completed. Pro-active policing carries the fight to the enemy, and can forestall criminal activity. Stings, reviewed in the last chapter, are examples of pro-active police work. Here we'll examine more vigorous measures.

One time-honored crime control tactic is to expel undesirables. Traditionally, the town sheriff or marshal confronted street criminals and ordered them to get out of town. Today's litigious civil-rights climate puts a damper on such active measures, yet they sometimes still take place.

The Los Angeles Police Department has for decades sought to keep organized crime off its turf. During the 1930s and 1940s detectives assigned to the organized crime unit watched train stations and turned back arriving mobsters. If verbal persuasion didn't work, they'd administer beatings to adjust the mobsters' attitudes. During the 1960s, officers would meet arriving mobsters at the airport and make it clear to them that they were unwelcome. By this time, beatings had stopped, and verbal dissuasion was enough to persuade the newcomers to turn around immediately. Darryl Gates, former Los Angeles Police Chief, admitted that such tactics are out of place during the last decade of the 20th Century because of "civil-rights" litigation.[1]

Political Investigations

Police agencies often have occasion to investigate politicians and their shortcomings. Even the smallest small-town police chief sometimes has to stop the mayor's son driving drunk down Main Street. At times, it's the mayor himself. In such cases, politics intervenes, and the local officer has to discreetly drive the mayor home. However, in true American-style politicking, the deed goes on deposit in the officer's "favor bank" to be redeemed when he needs it.

Contrary to the protests of liberal civil-rights advocates, investigating city and state politicians is legitimate police work, even if they're not under suspicion of a street crime. A simple and understandable fact of life is that a mayor, governor, or state legislator is not going to stick up a gas station. There are less risky ways to earn illicit money.

Like other people, some politicians lead double lives. Walter Jenkins, one of President Lyndon Johnson's White House staffers, was arrested in a Washington toilet for homosexuality. This wasn't his first arrest. Massachusetts Congressman Barney Frank's roommate ran a male prostitution ring from the apartment they shared. Many other federal legislators have been involved in scandals relating to alcoholism, illicit sex, financial wrongdoings, etc. From this it's obvious that politicians are prime targets for investigation because they have both the opportunities and propensities for illegal acts.

The Los Angeles Police Department, charged with policing California's most populous city, regularly investigates politicians, entertainers, and other high-profile people because of their proximity to organized crime figures. Politicians are always desirable people to bribe. Movers and shakers behind the scenes are often making private arrangements outside the law. The entertainment industry has a solid record of affiliations with organized crime, and many entertainers are involved in illicit sex or drugs. When an investigation takes place, it necessarily involves the subject's known associates, who may be part of the crime.

There have been recent investigations of Los Angeles Mayor Tom Bradley, Congressmen

Edward Roybal and Mervyn Dymally, Councilman Richard Alatorre, State Senator Art Torres, and others. One author has labeled these "fishing expeditions."[2] It's clear that such investigations are justified, given the well-documented corruption prevalent in American politics. The alternative is for police to put on blinders and refuse to investigate possible criminal involvement by the high and mighty because they are above the law.

Counter-Insurgency

Police conducting counter-intelligence or counter-insurrection programs generally have more freedom of action than ordinary officers. There may be an "emergency" declared, and a suspension of civil rights and ordinary criminal justice procedures. Also, police in such instances develop a siege mentality, justifying extreme measures.

An important point is that totalitarian secret-police methods are not the monopoly of dictatorships. There have been "killer-squad" hits undertaken by British S.A.S. troopers during the Northern Ireland War in recent years. S.A.S. troopers are a far cry from the conventional unarmed and friendly British "Bobbies," and the British government justified such harsh methods by citing the violence of the Irish Republican Army.

Police methods can become very extreme during "emergencies," when both the police and its government feel that the survival of the nation is at stake. American anti-war organizations during the Vietnam Era came under surveillance by local police, the FBI, and Army Intelligence, as well as other military organizations. The government's concern was that peace organizations were communist fronts, and they strove to uncover connections with foreign governments. With all that, the Vietnam Era protests and government reactions were relatively peaceful, despite a few unintentional deaths such as the Kent State University shootings. For examples of heavy-handed and lethal police actions, we have to look to foreign shores. The British counter-insurgency in Malaya during the late 1940s provides an example of how a "democratic" Western government and its police organizations can pull out all the stops when the struggle takes place away from home, and the insurgents are non-Caucasians.

Case Study: "The Officer From Special Branch"

Typically, secret-police methods and tactics fall under a cover of deep secrecy, often never to see the light of day. A few accounts surface, usually provided by the victims of the police, but many dismiss their statements as propaganda. The occasional renegade police officer discloses some of the events after his retirement, when he's beyond the reach of agency discipline. Some topics, and some wars, remain hot potatoes decades after their end and anyone who makes state secrets public risks prosecution. This is especially true in Great Britain, where the "Official Secrets Act" allows prosecution of anyone who reveals classified information, however obtained.

This is why some British Intelligence officers have gone abroad to publish their memoirs. A recent one was Peter Wright, author of *Spycatcher,* who had his memoirs published in Australia and the United States. Another was the individual who used the pen name "Tom Lilley," who appears to have been a British police officer serving during the Malayan insurrection. Lilley published his disclosures in the form of a novel, probably to avoid lawsuits from British police officers who actually served in Malaya and used the methods outlined in Lilley's book. The foreword stated that none of the methods described were actually used by the authorities in Malaya, that all characters are fictional, and that the novel is set in a fictional Malayan state. These multiple disclaimers almost guarantee that the story is thinly disguised fact, and that police tactics and stratagems described reflected reality.[3]

The first police dirty trick described is the arrest and interrogation of five suspected communist underground leaders. The local head of "Special Branch," the British political and secret police, arranged for every adult in the village where the five suspects lived to be interrogated for four minutes each as part of the deception plan. The first of the five suspects to arrive at the police station, however, would undergo a five-hour interrogation, after which he'd be released while police arrested the other four suspects. The

Special Branch head calculated that this would give the impression that the arrests resulted from information provided by the man they'd interrogated and released, and that fear of arrest might stampede other communist guerrillas into trying to escape. A side-effect was that the communists would seek revenge on the man they'd been led to believe had betrayed them. This gruesome prospect did not disturb the head Special Branch officer. His only worry was that there might be no attempt on this suspect's life, which would suggest that his information had been wrong.

The operation went as planned, and several previously unsuspected communists ran into ambushes in trying to sneak out of the village one night. The man whom the police had set up as the putative informer was shot to death at a barbershop, and his killers cut out his tongue to connote that he'd died for informing.

Another trick, undertaken early in the story, was to booby-trap any abandoned communist guerrilla camps British troops discovered. This was better than total destruction upon discovery because it became possible to destroy some guerrillas as well, instead of merely physical property. To lure a communist guerrilla unit into the booby-trapped camp, Special Branch officers arranged for a forged order from the communist high command to reach the leader of a particular guerrilla company. An anti-communist volunteer would bring the note to the communist troops, and to lend realism to the effort, there would be a faked fire-fight with British troops in the area.

The fake communist guerrilla would have a surgical wound in his leg to simulate a bullet wound. The plan worked, and when the guerrillas occupied the camp, British sappers detonated the mines, killing almost all of the communist unit. Their commander, however, escaped unhurt.

The Special Branch devised another plan to capture the guerrilla leader by blackmailing his brother, a schoolteacher who kept a mistress on the side. They persuaded the brother to lure the guerrilla commander into a trap, and this was where Special Branch officers and British troops captured him.

British troops occasionally discovered guerrilla supply dumps, and this gave Special Branch further opportunities. The plan was to sabotage or adulterate communist supplies, instead of destroying them. Special Branch officers knew that one guerrilla leader was diabetic, and when they discovered a stockpile of insulin, they diluted the liquid in the vials so that the leader would fall ill. This was preferable to inserting poison, which would kill him. The reasoning was that, if the guerrilla leader died, the communist high command would merely replace him. By diluting his insulin, they'd keep him partly incapacitated and less able to carry out his duties.

Another wrinkle in the sabotage plan was to contaminate communist rice stockpiles with bamboo hairs. These are very fine, and almost invisible. When ingested, they become embedded in the stomach walls because of their fish-hook shape, and cause chronic inflammation which is practically incurable.

Starting Wars

A police intelligence unit can sometimes take advantage of an opportunity to instigate a gang war between rival criminal factions. If there already exists a dispute over territory, sharing the trade, or other issues, a careful "hit" made to look like the handiwork of a rival gang can provoke reprisals.

The crucial factor is that tension and distrust between the two target groups be so high that denials of guilt won't be credible. With both sides poised for war, it doesn't take much to light the spark.

Notes:

1. *L.A. Secret Police,* Mike Rothmiller and Ivan G. Goldman, NY, Pocket Books, 1992, pp. 143-144.
2. *Ibid.,* pp. 156-157.
3. *The Officer From Special Branch,* Tom Lilley, NY, Doubleday & Company, Inc., 1971, "Foreword" p. 7.

12
Finale

Methods such as these help police fight fire with fire. Our outnumbered police officers, confronted by street-smart gangsters who openly flout the rules and know all the tricks, need an edge to avoid being swamped by dangerous law-breakers. At times, breaking the rules and using extra-legal methods provide the needed edge.

13
For Further Reading

A Speeder's Guide to Avoiding Tickets, Sgt. James M. Eagan, N.Y.S.P. (Ret.) NY, Avon Books, 1990. *This is a very easy-to-read guide to traffic ticket survival, written by an experienced state trooper.*

Badge of Betrayal, Joe Cantlupe & Lisa Petrillo, NY, Avon Books, 1991. *This book recounts the story of an investigation by police into the deadly conduct of another person wearing the badge. It tells of how investigators finally apprehended the* *officer who went bad, using common investigative methods, including the good cop/bad cop technique.*

By Way of Deception, Victor Ostrovsky and Claire Hoy, NY, St. Martin's Paperbacks, 1991. *The author uncovers the successes and especially the failures of the Israeli spy and covert action network. These accounts allow us to see what can go wrong in secret actions, and to draw lessons from other people's failures.*

City Police, Jonathan Rubinstein, NY, Ballantine Books, 1973. *The author rode with Philadelphia police officers until they got so used to him that he became part of their background, and they acted as if he wasn't there. This provided a crucial and eloquent insight into how cops really think and act.*

Criminal Victimization in the United States, 1990, U.S. Department of Justice, Bureau of Justice Statistics, February, 1992. Report NCJ-134126. *This report is the alternative to the FBI Uniform Crime Reports, and is based on a sampling of Americans across the country, not just those who report crimes to police. One surprising finding of this series is that the trend in crime rates has been downward since 1973, although reported crimes have tended to increase. Apparently, although there are now somewhat* *fewer crimes, somewhat more people are reporting them.*

Family Of Spies, Pete Earley, NY, Bantam Books, 1988. Family of Spies *provides a look at how FBI counter-espionage agents conduct investigations. Reading between the lines shows that there are many spy cases incomplete or undetected.*

Interrogation, Burt Rapp, Port Townsend, WA, Loompanics Unlimited, 1987. *A good book that provides a comprehensive, no-holds-barred look at what really happens in interrogations.*

Interrogation: Techniques of the Royal Canadian Mounted Police, Anonymous, Boulder, CO, Paladin Press, 1991. *This text provides many tricks and deceptions for cajoling a confession from a suspect.*

L.A. Secret Police, Mike Rothmiller and Ivan G. Goldman, NY, Pocket Books, 1992. *The authors tell of the secret methods used by a secret unit of the LAPD. Some methods are unattractive, but the LAPD has had to deal with some very unattractive and unsavory lawbreakers.*

Law Enforcement News, NY, John Jay College of Criminal Justice. *This is the most objective law enforcement publication in the country because it's not connected with any police agency and does not run advertisements by suppliers of police* *equipment. The editorial slant is on the liberal side, but the reporting is both accurate and comprehensive.*

Merchants of Treason, Thomas B. Allen & Norman Polmar, NY, Delacorte Press, 1988. *This book also provides a look at the no-holds-barred world of counter-espionage, where a variety of dirty tricks are both justifiable and legal.*

Privacy For Sale, Jeffrey Rothfeder, NY, Simon & Schuster, 1992. *The world of computer espionage and information-gathering is widespread and frightening. In fact, the biggest violators are not police agencies, who have their hands too full with dangerous lawbreakers to bother peeping at innocent citizens, but commercial data-collectors, who gather a variety of privileged information about Americans for crassly commercial purposes.*

The FBI-KGB War, Robert J. Lamphere and Tom Shactman, NY, Berkley Books, 1987. *Lamphere's book gives us an inside view of how the counter-espionage effort of the 1940s and 1950s was run by the FBI. The raw information is both startling and enlightening.*

The Mugging, Morton Hunt, NY, Signet Books, 1972. *This account of a mugging also provides chapters on topics such as police interrogation techniques.*

The Officer From Special Branch, Tom Lilley, NY, Doubleday & Company, Inc., 1971. *This is a fictional representation of real-life events, with locale and author disguised to prevent reprisals.*

Sourcebook of Criminal Justice Statistics — 1990, Washington, DC, U.S. Department of Justice, Bureau of Criminal Justice Statistics, 1991. *Each annual in this series provides a comprehensive look at the crime picture in this country, and an interesting outline of various branches of the criminal justice system.*

The Squad, Michael Milan, NY, Berkley Books, 1992. The Squad *is a surprisingly frank and unofficial look at how a low-profile police intelligence unit really operates. This book isn't a glorification of the unit, but an account of both successes and failures, with the emphasis on how personalities and politics often impede the unit's effectiveness.*

Surreptitous Entry, Willis George, Boulder, CO, Paladin Press, 1990. *George's book is a classic on black bag jobs, and how the government used them against both civil lawbreakers and foreign agents.*

A Tremor in the Blood, David Thoreson Lykken, NY, McGraw-Hill, 1981. *This is the authoritative book on the polygraph and other gadgets and gimmicks touted as "lie detectors." The author also* *deals with honesty tests and shows how and why they are ineffective.*

Under Cover: Police Surveillance in America, Gary T. Marx, Berkeley, CA, University of California Press, 1988. Under Cover *is a collection of accounts of how police surveillance methods go wrong, often citing abuses, and how not to do it. This is a good text on how not to do it.*

Index